T0319060

Cambridge Elements

Elements in Psychology and Culture
edited by
Kenneth D. Keith
University of San Diego

ACCULTURATION

A Personal Journey across Cultures

John W. Berry
Queen's University, Kingston, Canada
Higher School of Economics, Moscow, Russian Federation

CAMBRIDGE
UNIVERSITY PRESS

University Printing House, Cambridge CB2 8BS, United Kingdom

One Liberty Plaza, 20th Floor, New York, NY 10006, USA

477 Williamstown Road, Port Melbourne, VIC 3207, Australia

314–321, 3rd Floor, Plot 3, Splendor Forum, Jasola District Centre, New Delhi – 110025, India

79 Anson Road, #06–04/06, Singapore 079906

Cambridge University Press is part of the University of Cambridge.

It furthers the University's mission by disseminating knowledge in the pursuit of education, learning, and research at the highest international levels of excellence.

www.cambridge.org
Information on this title: www.cambridge.org/9781108731096
DOI: 10.1017/9781108589666

First published 2019

A catalogue record for this publication is available from the British Library.

ISBN 978-1-108-73109-6 Paperback
ISSN 2515-3986 (online)
ISSN 2515-3943 (print)

Acculturation

A Personal Journey across Cultures

Elements in Psychology and Culture

DOI: 10.1017/9781108589666
First published online: August 2019

John W. Berry
Queen's University, Kingston, Canada
Higher School of Economics, Moscow, Russian Federation

Author for correspondence: John W. Berry, elderberrys@gmail.com

Abstract: Acculturation is the process of group and individual changes in culture and behaviour that result from intercultural contact. These changes have been taking place forever, and continue at an increasing pace as more and more peoples of different cultures move, meet and interact. Variations in the meanings of the concept and some systematic conceptualizations of it are presented. This is followed by a survey of empirical work with indigenous, immigrant and ethnocultural peoples around the globe that employed both ethnographic (qualitative) and psychological (quantitative) methods. This wide-ranging research has been undertaken in a quest for possible general principles (or universals) of acculturation. This Element concludes with a short evaluation of the field of acculturation and its past, present and future.

Keywords: acculturation, adaptation, culture, ethnicity, immigrants, Indigenous Peoples, intercultural contact, refugees, wellbeing

ISBNs: 9781108731096 (PB), 9781108589666 (OC)
ISSNs: 2515-3986 (online), 2515-3943 (print)

Contents

1 Introduction

Although peoples have moved across continents and borders since human beings first appeared, the world is currently experiencing very large population flows due to political, economic, ecological and military events. The psychological, cultural and political impact on these arriving populations is profound, as are the impacts on those societies which receive them. These events make the study and understanding of why people move, how they engage each other and their eventual settlement a matter of urgency for social and behavioural scientists, and for policy and programme developers.

This Element seeks to provide some concepts and empirical findings that may contribute to this understanding, and perhaps also to more successful policies, programmes and outcomes for all groups and individuals involved. Two research domains (*acculturation* and *intercultural relations*) have developed markedly in recent years (see Berry, 2017; Sam & Berry, 2016) and provide a base on which we may be able to achieve such understanding and positive outcomes.

From early in the appearance of human beings, all the world's peoples have been in contact with cultural others. Although there must have been just one starting point for the human species, the cultural diversification of populations began to appear due to two fundamental factors: *adaptation to ecological context* and *acculturation due to intercultural contact* (Fagan & Durani, 2016). These two features have shaped human life up until the present time, and are basic to understanding the diversity of human behaviour (Berry, 2018, 2019).

Variations in these phenomena began with variations in ecological settings that induced cultural adaptations (Boyd & Richerson, 2005). These constantly evolving habitats and continuing changes in them (brought about by human activity, natural catastrophes and moving to new locations) require changing responses by human groups and individuals. Second, contacts with other cultures, whether through colonization, immigration or other kinds of intercultural engagements, induced acculturation, bringing further cultural changes (Redfield, Linton & Herskovits, 1936) and individual behavioural changes (Graves, 1967; Sam & Berry, 2016).

This line of thought runs through this Element: ecology and contact ➔ differing cultural adaptations ➔ variations and changes in behavioural development and expression. In any account of human cultural and psychological variation, these two exogenous factors (ecology and contact) need to be conceptualized and assessed, and then linked to cultural and psychological outcomes for groups and individuals. Ecological adaptation sets the stage, while intercultural contact demands further adaptations through the process of acculturation.

Where did these ideas come from? While I have learned (Berry, 1995) from Feldman (1975) and Jahoda (1995) that these ideas had a long history in anthropological and psychological thought, my initial orientation to research stemmed from my own personal experiences, rather than from the academic literature. These early experiences have been outlined (Berry, 1997a) in a kind of academic autobiography, where I identified personal experiences and circumstances (both ecological and sociopolitical) that shaped my views about human behaviour in general.

I grew up in a French-speaking village in rural Quebec, as a member of the only English-speaking family living there. This village was adjacent to a Mohawk community. Daily contact with the 'others' had a profound impact on my views about human diversity and the cultural and psychological variations that accompanied this diversity. Later, during summers while in high school, I worked in the bush alongside Algonquian and French *bucheron*, and then as a merchant seaman in Canada. I continued working at sea for a few more years, first working on a Norwegian ship along the coast of Africa (Angola, Belgian Congo, South Africa, Mozambique and Mauritius). I then signed on as an engineer on a marine biology research ship in the Canadian Arctic, visiting many Cree and Inuit communities in Hudson Bay and James Bay. These all became community research sites for many years thereafter. When confronted by the choice ('the sea or me') from my future wife, I then came ashore to work as an upholsterer in a factory, and then as a stock clerk for a manufacturer of wine and beer bottles (containing the essential ingredients of a happy life) in Montreal, working alongside mostly immigrant colleagues.

During this latter period, I began to take night courses at Sir George Williams University in Montreal, from which I received a BA in 1963. Most of my courses in psychology were taught by James W. Bridges, who had been born in 1885 in the small province of Prince Edward Island, and who received his PhD at Harvard in 1913, under the direction of Hugo Munsterberg. Since Munsterberg had received his PhD under Wundt, I can claim some apostolic (academic) succession to that great man! Bridges had been trained as a psychologist, and had helped to devise the Army Alpha and Beta intelligence tests (Yerkes, Bridges & Hardwick, 1917). He also later trained as an anthropologist and, with his friend and colleague Otto Klineberg, he promoted the importance of linking these two disciplines. Bridges usually inserted the phrase 'in our culture' in his lectures in order to limit the claims to generality of any psychological finding being reported. Bridges showed me the way to think of psychology as a culturally embedded and global discipline, rather than as one that was limited to a small part of the world.

Although graduating from a little-known university, I was accepted by Professor James Drever to do a PhD at the University of Edinburgh. At the time, Drever was President of the International Union of Psychological Sciences (1963–6; following Otto Klineberg, 1960–3), and was spearheading the development of the *International Journal of Psychology*. He encouraged me to pursue the broader international vision instilled by Bridges, and was very supportive of my carrying out fieldwork away from Edinburgh in Africa, in the Arctic and in northern Scotland.

In summary, these personal experiences and academic influences made it imperative that I confront the Eurocentric bias of Western Academic Scientific Psychology (WASP) and become a cross-cultural psychologist. I knew intuitively that a research finding somewhere, at some time, and with just some people, could not be a valid basis of understanding human behaviour in all its diversity. My goal has been to contribute to the achievement of a global psychology, one that incorporates psychological concepts and empirical findings from all the peoples of the world (Berry, 2013a), which may then serve as a valid basis for human betterment.

This Element is an account of, and a personal reflection on, the phenomena of acculturation viewed as part of the broader fields of cross-cultural and intercultural psychology. Both fields seek to understand the development and display of human behaviour in their cultural contexts. However, intercultural psychology focuses on behaviours that result from intercultural contact, mainly occurring in culturally diverse societies. In contrast, cross-cultural psychology requires independent cultural contexts in order to make valid comparisons and generalizations.

This Element does not aspire to be a systematic review of the field of acculturation psychology, which is of course now beyond the scope of any one person or publication.

1.1 Approach to Research

I have approached research guided by a few beliefs. The first is that I accept the philosophical perspectives of realism. That is, I accept that things actually exist, beyond our perception of them. They have qualities and characteristics that can be discovered and interpreted through the use of the scientific method. I reject any claim that 'there is no there there.'

Second, I accept that both individuals and societies exist as distinct entities, and do so at their own levels; one is not reducible to the other. As J. J. Rousseau opined: 'a thing called society exists outside the individual, as a mass of rules, relationships, injunctions and customs.' This conception means that societies and individuals need to be examined in their own right in any research project in cross-cultural or intercultural psychology. On the basis of their independent conceptual and empirical status, their relationships can then be examined and discovered.

Third, I have never had an overall plan or strategy for developing a research programme, other than seeking as much cultural variation as possible. However, I have had some guides to assist in deciding what to do, including having fun and being useful when doing research. These guides have also assisted in deciding what *not* to do; this is why I have never done an experiment or worked in a laboratory or clinic. One key focus has been my interest in understanding hunters and gatherers living in many parts of the world, and how they have dealt (both culturally and psychologically) with their colonization, subjugation, dispersal and relocation.

Fourth, I have adopted the method called *etak* that is used for navigation in Polynesia and Micronesia. This system uses observations of events (such as the sun, stars, currents, winds and clouds) in order to navigate successfully between islands. A key assumption of *etak* is that the island of destination itself moves and comes to the navigator (rather than the navigator moving to the island of destination). This conception has influenced my own research strategy: I have not set out on a voyage with a specific goal in mind. While I do have some principles and beliefs (as noted earlier), I lie in wait, seeking opportunities to come my way, just as the island of destination comes by in the *etak* system. This has meant that I have usually had a variety of research projects underway at the same time. This is a benefit, because when a barrier crops up, you can back off (or just anchor) and wait for another opportunity (island) to come your way.

My early and continuing involvement in the fields of cross-cultural and intercultural psychology has been the foundation of my professional life. My aim has been to be 'first in, last out'. I have published in the first volumes of the *International Journal of Psychology* (1966) and the *Journal of Cross-Cultural Psychology* (1970). I have continued this programme of publications up until now, submitting my international work to international journals and books and my Canadian research to Canadian journals and books. I have not submitted any to US journals, because I do not do research there. My few publications in those journals were either invited or were done to assist colleagues there in promoting the fields of cross-cultural and intercultural psychology. Many colleagues advised me that my decision to publish in this way would never lead to a successful academic career.

1.2 Ecocultural Framework

My main theoretical perspective is the ecocultural approach to cross-cultural and intercultural psychology. I first outlined this in my PhD thesis (Berry,

1966a), and it was first published in Berry (1966b, 1967, 1976). I developed this approach to use as a guide to studying the contrasting perceptual skills, cognitive abilities and social attributes of hunting/gathering and agricultural populations, and later as a framework for consolidations of the field of cross-cultural psychology (e.g., Berry et al., 2011). As noted earlier, acculturation (resulting from intercultural contact) has been an integral component in the ecocultural framework from the beginning of my research, along with these ecological influences on behaviour.

At its core, the ecocultural approach combines the ecological, cultural and intercultural perspectives on understanding the development and display of human behaviour. This perspective considers that all group and individual features of human populations can only be understood when situated in their contexts. The *ecological* approach examines phenomena in their natural contexts (habitats) and attempts to identify relationships between the cultural and behavioural phenomena and these contexts. The *cultural* approach examines individual behaviours in the cultural contexts in which they develop and are displayed. When these examinations are carried out comparatively, the *cross-cultural* approach results. When these are carried out with populations that are in contact with each other, the *intercultural* approach results. Essential to understanding all these approaches are the concepts of *interaction* and *adaptation*. Interaction implies reciprocal relationships among elements in the system; adaptation implies that changes take place that may (or may not) increase their mutual fit or compatibility within the system.

In addition to this ecology ➔ culture ➔ behaviour line of thinking, another line in the ecocultural framework originates from contact with other cultures. This second source of influence links the *sociopolitical* context that brings about contact with other cultures, which in turn shapes both the original ecological and cultural features of the group and then the behaviour of individuals in the group. In this case, there are both interactions among peoples of diverse cultural backgrounds, and mutual adaptations to intercultural contact. This second line of relationships is now widely studied using the concept of *acculturation*. Research on the impact on cultures and individuals from contact with outside cultures has been advancing greatly in recent years (Sam & Berry, 2006/2016). This domain has come to the fore because of the dramatic increases in intercultural contact, migration, globalization and culture change (Berry, 1980a, 2008).

By combining the ecological and sociopolitical sources of influence on how groups and individuals develop, interact and adapt to change, the ecocultural approach to understanding human behaviour is generated. Its core claims are that cultural and biological features of human populations interact with, and are adaptive to, both the ecological and sociopolitical contexts in which they develop and live, and that the development and display of individual human behaviour are adaptive to these contexts.

To operationalize this ecocultural perspective, an ecocultural research *framework* was developed, starting in the 1960s (Berry, 1966a, 1966b). This framework has evolved through a series of conceptual elaborations and empirical studies devoted to understanding similarities and differences in perceptual, cognitive and social behaviours in relation to their ecological, cultural and intercultural contexts (Berry, 1967, 1976, 1979; Berry, van de Koppel et al., 1986; Georgas, Berry, van de Vijver, Kagitcibasi & Poortinga, 2006; Mishra & Berry, 2017; Mishra, Sinha & Berry, 1996). The ecocultural approach has also been used as an organizing framework in a series of books that seeks to integrate the vast field of cross-cultural psychology (Berry, Poortinga, Breugelmans, Chasiotis & Sam, 2011; Berry, Poortinga, Segall & Dasen, 1992, 2002; Segall, Dasen, Berry & Poortinga, 1990, 1999).

In more detail, the ecocultural framework (see Figure 1.1) seeks to account for human psychological diversity (both group and individual similarities and differences) by considering the two fundamental sources of influence noted earlier: *ecological* and *sociopolitical*. In adaptation to these contexts, two features of human populations (*cultural* and *biological* characteristics) become established in the group. These population variables are then transmitted to individuals by various *transmission* variables such as *enculturation, socialization, genetics* and *acculturation*. The outcomes of these exogenous variables impacting cultural and biological adaptations are then transmitted to individuals as the development of behaviours. These can be directly observed, and from these observations, we can make inferences as to the presence of underlying psychological characteristics.

The use of this framework to study and compare groups and individuals is made possible by the presence of shared cultural and psychological universals in all humanity. Without such commonalities, no research using common concepts and instruments, or any comparisons, would be possible. This position, known as *universalism*, maintains that: (1) all human beings share *basic* cultural features and psychological processes; and (ii) cultures and behaviours become developed and expressed in varying ways, generating the *surface* variability that can be observed in everyday life.

This ecocultural framework provides a broad structure within which to examine the development and expression of similarities and differences in human psychological functioning (both at individual and at group levels) by considering two main contexts: ecology and sociopolitical influences. That is, the framework considers human diversity (both cultural and psychological) to

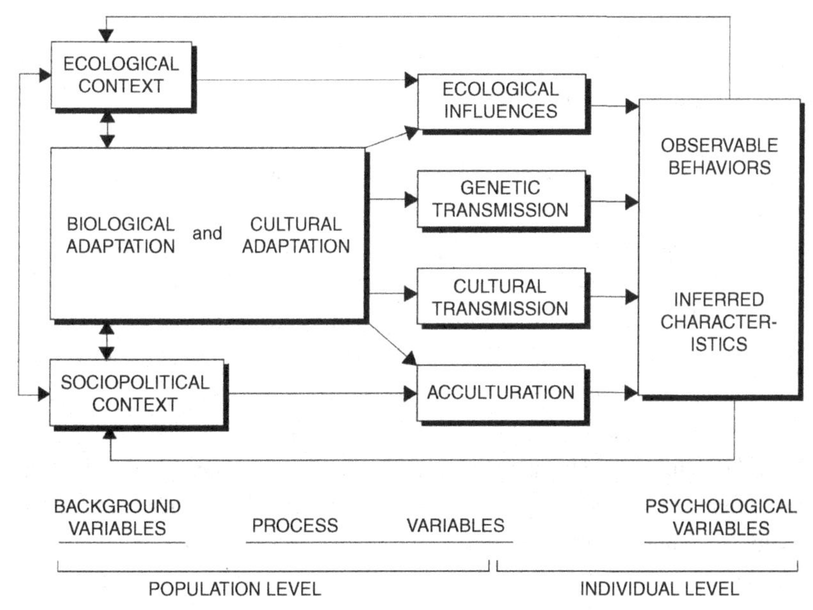

Figure 1.1 The ecocultural framework (modified from Berry, 1976)

be a set of collective and individual adaptations to context. Within this general perspective, it views cultures as evolving adaptations to ecological and socio-political influences and psychological characteristics in a population as adaptive to their cultural context as well as to the broader ecological and sociopolitical influences. The ecocultural perspective argues that, together, ecological and sociopolitical influences can be held to account for behavioural development and expression. Note that while the arrows linking components within the framework move from left to right (from exogenous contexts to behaviour), the relationships are usually interactive, with mutual influence changing both elements in the relationship. For example, human behaviour impacts the habitat of the group, and contact between groups alters the cultural characteristics of both groups. The upper and lower arrows that feed back to the exogenous contexts are intended to signify these mutual relationships within the framework.

1.2.1 Ecology → Culture Link

Relationships between ecology and culture have been postulated for a long time in anthropology, as noted by Feldman (1975) and Jahoda (1995). The claim that culture is adaptive to ecology has roots that go back to Forde's (1934) classic analysis of relationships between physical habitat and societal features of cultures in Africa. In that work, Forde examined 16 cultural groups, classifying them as food gatherers, cultivators or pastoral nomads. He was able to demonstrate 'complex relationships between the human habitat and the manifold technical and social devices for its exploitation', as well as other social and political features of their cultures (Forde, 1934, p. 460).

This theme of cultural adaptation to habitat asserts that cultural variations may be understood as long-term adaptations to differing ecological settings or contexts (Boyd & Richerson, 1983). This line of thinking is known variously as cultural ecology (Vayda & Rappaport, 1968), ecological anthropology (Moran, 2006) or environmental anthropology (Townsend, 2009). These ideas are closely related to the theory of cultural materialism (Harris, 1968). Note that these views are unlike earlier simplistic assumptions about how the environment *determined* culture and behaviour (e.g., the school of 'environmental determinism'; Huntington, 1945). Instead, the ecological school of thinking in anthropology has ranged from the notion of *possibilism* (where the environment sets some constraints on, or limits the range of, possible cultural forms that may emerge) to an emphasis on *resource utilization* (where active and interactive relationships between human populations and their habitats are examined in relation to the resources available, such as water, soil and temperature).

1.2.2 Ecology → Biology Link

The links between habitat and biology go back at least to Darwin (1859) and continue to this day. Species and their individual members adapt through a process of natural selection that allows adaptive traits to survive and to be passed on over generations. This line of thinking parallels that of culture as adaptive to ecological context, and takes place in tandem with it. In the ecocultural framework, biology and culture are seen as complementary ways in which populations adapt to their habitats. The growing study of how biology and culture both play a role in ontogenetic development has been outlined by Keller (2011). An evolutionary approach to this culture–biology relationship has been emphasized in recent work (Boyd, Richerson & Henrich, 2011) where the two are viewed as jointly changing in response to habitat change.

1.2.3 Ecology → Culture → Behaviour Link

The linking of human behavioural development to cultural and biological adaptation, and thence back to ecology, has an equally long history in psychology (Berry, 1995; Jahoda, 1995). Contemporary thinking about this sequence (ecology-culture-behaviour) is often traced to the work of Kardiner and colleagues (e.g., Kardiner & Linton, 1939). They proposed that *primary institutions* (such as subsistence economic and socialization practices) lead to *basic personality structures*, which in turn lead to *secondary institutions* (such as art, governance, religion and play). In this sequence, there are ecological beginnings with cultural and then psychological outcomes. This sequence may form a feedback loop in which the evolved behaviours return to influence the ecological and cultural settings in which they emerged. This line of thinking served as a basis for the work of John and Beatrice Whiting (Whiting & Whiting, 1975) in the development of their psychocultural perspective. With respect to transmission, our understanding of both cultural and genetic transmissions has been strongly advanced by work on culture learning (e.g., Keller, 2002) and cultural transmission (Schönpflug, 2009).

1.2.4 Sociopolitical Context → Culture → Behaviour Link

At the lower level of the model, contact with other cultures is a major exogenous influence on the cultures and behaviours. These contacts have come about as a result of exploration and colonization of Indigenous Peoples, by enslavement and by the movements of refugees and immigrants. The features of a culture and the behaviours of individuals within it are both transformed by these external influences. This means that individuals must now adapt to more than one cultural context. When many cultural contexts are involved (as in situations of multiple culture contacts over years), psychological phenomena can be viewed as attempts to deal simultaneously and successively with two or more (sometimes inconsistent, sometimes conflicting) cultural contexts. Such contact brings about cultural and biological change in the population, and initiates the process of psychological acculturation. Research on these various sociopolitical influences on culture and behaviour has come to dominate much of the fields of cross-cultural and intercultural psychology in recent years (Berry et al., 2011; Sam & Berry, 2016).

1.2.5 Ecology → Sociopolitical Contexts Link

The two main exogenous variables in the framework (ecology and sociopolitical contexts) are not independent of each other. This is because of two factors. First, contact between cultures (mainly due to colonization, but also due to migration) is influenced by the habitats of both the source and the destination. Some locales are ecologically degraded, from which people flee, and some are attractive for colonization and settlement. The presence of resources (such as minerals, water and arable land for agriculture) have influenced where people have invaded, migrated and settled. Second, the impact of colonization and settlement on resident populations has been variable: those with a highly structured political and military organizations are more able to resist occupation and domination. Related to this is psychological evidence (e.g., Berry, 1976) showing that hunter/gatherers (which are usually smaller-scale societies with limited political structures to deal with the demands of invaders) have been more negatively impacted by acculturation pressures than more politically structured societies. Thus, we can claim that these two major inputs are related to each other and interact in ways that produce a complex pattern and flow across the ecocultural framework.

Over time, the ecocultural framework has been elaborated. I (1966b, 1971) originally called my framework an 'ecological-cultural-behavioural' model (later shortened to 'ecocultural' in 1976). Bronfenbrenner (1979) named his approach 'ecological', and the Whitings (Whiting & Whiting, 1975) referred to their approach as 'psychocultural', and also used the concept of the 'ecological niche'. Super and Harkness (1986, 1997) coined the term 'developmental niche', and Weisner (1984) continued the use of the term 'ecocultural'. All of these approaches attempt to understand the development and display of human behaviour as a function of the process of group and individual adaptation to ecological, cultural, biological and sociopolitical (intercultural) settings.

To summarize, the ecological and sociopolitical lines of influence have equal conceptual status as factors in the development and display of human behaviour. The actual degree of influence of each factor is variable across settings, populations and individuals. The inclusion of the sociopolitical line in the ecocultural framework sets the stage for a more detailed examination of the processes and outcomes of acculturation.

2 Acculturation

2.1 Definition of Acculturation

Acculturation is the process of cultural and psychological change that takes place as a result of contact between two or more cultural groups and their individual members. At the cultural group level, it involves changes in social structures and institutions and in cultural norms (Redfield et al., 1936). At the individual psychological level, it involves changes in people's behavioural repertoires (including their food, dress, language, values and identities) and their eventual adaptation to these intercultural encounters (Thurnwald, 1932). Acculturation is a mutual process in which these changes take place in all groups and individuals in contact. The concept is also complex and multifaceted (Rudmin, 2009) with widely varying definitions (Ward, 2001). Despite this complexity, two formulations of the concept of acculturation have been widely quoted, and remain a foundation for the field. The first is:

> Acculturation comprehends those phenomena which result when groups of individuals having different cultures come into continuous first-hand contact, with subsequent changes in the original culture patterns of either or both groups . . . under this definition, acculturation is to be distinguished from culture change, of which it is but one aspect, and assimilation, which is at times a phase of acculturation. (Redfield et al., 1936, pp. 149–52)

In another formulation, acculturation was defined as:

> culture change that is initiated by the conjunction of two or more autonomous cultural systems. Acculturative change may be the consequence of direct cultural transmission; it may be derived from non-cultural causes, such as ecological or demographic modification induced by an impinging culture; it may be delayed, as with internal adjustments following upon the acceptance of alien traits or patterns; or it may be a reactive adaptation of traditional modes of life. (Social Science Research Council, 1954, p. 974).

In the first formulation, acculturation is seen as one aspect of the broader concept of culture change (one that results from intercultural contact), is considered to generate change in 'either or both groups' and is distinguished from assimilation (which may be 'at times a phase' of acculturation). These are important distinctions for psychological work and are pursued later in this Element. In the second definition, a few extra features are added: change can be *indirect* (not cultural, but 'ecological', due to alteration in habitat); *delayed* (there can be a cultural and psychological lag, which can result in change years after contact); and sometimes 'reactive' (i.e., groups and individuals may reject the 'outside' cultural influences and change back towards a more 'traditional' way of life, rather than inevitably towards greater similarity with the dominant culture).

Graves (1967) introduced the concept of *psychological acculturation*. This concept refers to changes in an individual who is a participant in a culture-contact situation, being influenced both directly by the external culture and by the changing culture of which the individual is a member. At this individual level, the kinds of changes taking place might be in identity, values, attitudes or behaviour. Both the cultural and psychological levels of acculturation need to be studied in any comprehensive examination of how groups and individuals change following intercultural contact.

It is clear that the relationships between these two levels need to be examined, for two reasons. First, cultural changes in the group set the stage for psychological changes in individuals; an understanding of the cultural context is required in order to accurately describe and interpret the resultant psychological changes. Second, not all individuals undergo acculturation in the same way. Even in a common cultural context, individuals will not have the same motives or experiences; hence they may have different psychological consequences. Thus, there is no simple relationship between cultural and psychological features of acculturation: not every group or every individual engages the process in the same way or evidences the same outcomes.

2.2 Recent Variations in Conceptualizing Acculturation

Although these early definitions still serve as the basis for much work on acculturation, more recent dimensions have been proposed (Berry & Sam, 2016). First, it is no longer considered necessary for acculturation to be based on 'continuous first-hand' contact. With growing use of telemedia, acculturation may take place remotely, in line with earlier work on *cultural diffusion* (Berry, 1980a), in which aspects of culture flow across boundaries without actual intercultural contact. For example, research by Ferguson and Bornstein (2012) has shown that Jamaican youth are taking on US cultural and psychological attributes (even without ever having been in direct personal contact with that society) through a process they call remote acculturation. Rather, they are exposed to US culture through media and tourism.

The second new dimension examines acculturation that takes place over the long term. Rather than being a phenomenon that occurs only within the lifetime of an individual or in a few generations, acculturation can take place over centuries or even millennia. This phenomenon has been examined by Gezentsvey-Lamy, Ward and Liu (2013) with Jewish, Maori and Chinese samples. This longer time frame resembles the approach of modernization theory (Inkeles & Smith, 1974).

A third issue has become prominent with the increasing cultural diversity of national societies, where there is no longer one single dominant group with which ethnocultural groups can be in contact (van Oudenhoven & Ward, 2013). With multiple groups available in the larger society, the pattern of intercultural contacts becomes more complex. As a result, more ethnographic research becomes necessary in order to understand this increasingly complex network of intercultural relations. For example, Berry and Sabatier (2011) examined the acculturation of immigrant youth who had settled in Montreal, Canada. In this city, there are two dominant groups (French and English) with whom immigrants may be in contact, and with whom they may interact and acculturate.

A fourth new feature is that of contact within plural societies that results from large-scale internal migration between culturally disparate regions. For example, Gui, Zheng and Berry (2012) examined migrant worker acculturation with men moving from remote peasant villages to large metropolises in China. This phenomenon is also important within the Russian Federation (Lebedeva &

Tatarko, 2013), where individuals from other regions are moving to large cities and changing the cultural complexity of these metropolises.

Finally, as for other areas of psychological study, the perspective of social constructivism has begun to challenge the positivist tradition of research (Chirkov, 2009). From this perspective, behaviour is considered to be 'socially constructed' in day-to-day interactions with others, rather than being a 'given' that is available for direct empirical observation. I (2009) have argued that both the positivist and the constructivist perspectives are required for a comprehensive understanding of acculturation phenomena. This dual approach begins with using the more qualitative traditions of cultural anthropology, with its close observation of daily activity, and the interpretation of the meanings people assign to these activities ('thick description'; Geertz, 1973). Based on this qualitative information, more quantitative methods can be developed that draw from psychological science, using samples, interviews, tests and statistical analyses. The framework presented in Figure 3.1 makes this dual approach explicit, in which cultures are examined using ethnographic and related qualitative methods prior to and following their intercultural contact. Then, on the basis of this ethnographic research, more quantitative methods are used. This focus allows for the contexts to be understood and available for use in the interpretation of the psychological phenomena being studied with quantitative methods.

3 General Acculturation Framework

As we have seen, acculturation is a complex set of phenomena; it has many components and many relationships among them. Over the years, various frameworks have been proposed that identify the key components of acculturation and that provide some structure to these phenomena (Berry, 1970, 1974a, 1997b). Similar frameworks have been developed and elaborated by Navas, García, Sánchez, Rojas, Pumares and Fernández (2005; the Relative Extended Acculturation Model) and by Safdar, Choung and Lewis (2013; the Multidimensional Individual Difference Acculturation Model).

In this framework, acculturation begins with contact between cultural groups and their individual members. Then these contacts lead to both cultural and psychological changes. Finally, these changes eventually lead to various forms of adaptation. These components and relationships among them are illustrated in Figure 3.1. Note that while the arrows are shown as moving from the group level (on the left) towards the individual level (on the right), there is much evidence of reciprocal or mutual influence, in which individuals' actions change the groups of which they are members, and even change the external sources of

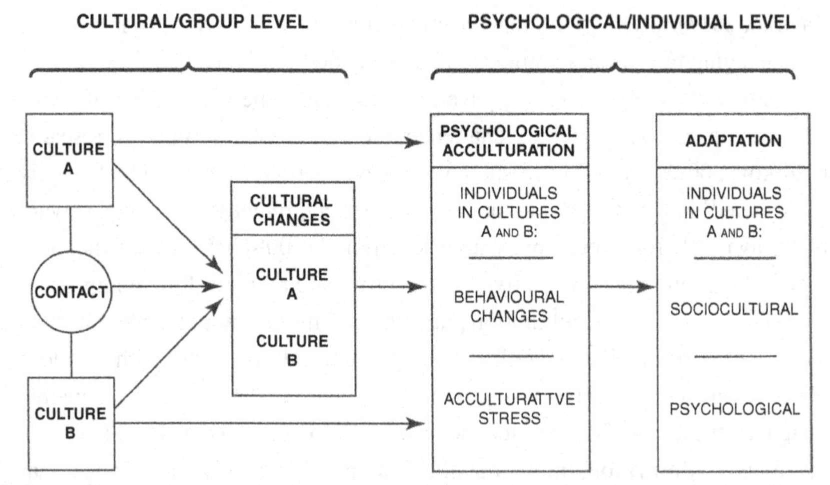

Figure 3.1 A framework for conceptualizing and studying acculturation (from Berry, 2003)

acculturation. This framework serves as a kind of map of those phenomena that I believe need to be conceptualized and measured during acculturation research.

At the cultural/group level (on the left), we need to understand key features of the two (or more) original *cultural groups* (A, B and so on) prior to their major contact. As noted earlier, the groups in contact have differential power, a factor which needs to be studied in order to understand the flow of acculturative influence among groups, and of the cultural changes that result in both groups. Typically, the dominant group serves as the 'larger society' (a term coined by George Manual, a leader of the National Indian Brotherhood in Canada in the 1970s) to refer to the broadly shared and evolving institutional framework in which all peoples attempt to live in a society. It is not the 'mainstream' which is usually only the dominant group's established way of living in the society. The non-dominant groups have culture as well, and are not simply 'minorities' which are small in number and power. Because all groups have cultural features that need to be studied, I have avoided using the concepts of 'mainstream' and 'minority' in my own work.

The ethnographic record is a good source for understanding the cultural features that are brought to the acculturation arena; ethnographic research on their current attributes may also be needed. The nature of their *contact relationships* (on the left, centre) needs to be investigated, including the purpose of their contact, such as colonization, economic or political domination or migration. To the right of these original cultures in contact are the resulting cultural changes in the groups as they emerge as *ethnocultural groups* during the process of acculturation. All cultural groups in contact change; no group is immune from this culture-change process, which can range from being rather easily accomplished (such as evolving a new economic base), through to being a source of major cultural disruption (such as becoming colonized and enslaved). These kinds of changes have been enumerated in detail in Berry, Trimble and Olmeda (1986).

At the individual level, we need to consider the *psychological acculturation* (in the middle of Figure 3.1) that individuals in all groups in contact undergo, and their eventual *adaptation* (on the right of Figure 3.1) to their new situations.

These psychological changes are the *what* component of individual acculturative changes; these are *behavioural changes, acculturative stress, acculturation strategies* and eventually various forms of *adaptation* (on the right).

3.1 Behavioural Changes

These can be a set of rather easily accomplished changes, including learning of new ones, or shedding of old ways of living. Virtually every aspect of an individual's behaviour is a candidate for change following intercultural contact, including the processes of culture learning and culture shedding (Berry, 1992). Studies have attended to a host of behaviours and psychological characteristics, but the most common are the usual daily activities (such as food, dress, social relationships) and more complex psychological features (such as abilities, cognitive styles, identities, values and personality).

There is no simple relation between how much contact there is (or the length of time of such contact) and the degree or kinds of behavioural changes that take place. The two main reasons for this complex relationship are the variations in acculturation strategies, and the experience of discrimination (to be discussed later in this Element).

3.2 Acculturative Stress

Changes can also be more challenging, even problematic. In such cases, the result may be an increase in *acculturative stress* as manifested by uncertainty, anxiety and depression (Berry, 2006a; Berry, Kim, Minde & Mok, 1987). These problematic aspects are at the core of concerns for the health and wellbeing of individuals engaged in the acculturation process.

The concept of acculturative stress was introduced by Berry (1970) and was defined as a special kind of response to the challenges of intercultural living. The concept was proposed as an alternative to the more widely used concept of *culture shock* (Oberg, 1960; Ward, Bochner & Furnham, 2001). The problem with the term *culture shock* is that *shock* is essentially a negative term, implying that only difficulties will result from culture contact. However, the term *stress* has a theoretical basis in studies of how people deal with challenges (called *stressors*) by engaging in various *coping* strategies, leading eventually to some form of adaptation (see Lazarus, 1997; Lazarus & Folkman, 1984). Within this acculturative stress perspective, people are seen as potentially able to deal effectively with stressors in their lives and to achieve a variety of outcomes (adaptations) ranging from very negative through to very positive (Berry, 2006a). Thus, from a stress (in contrast to a shock) perspective, acculturation contact experiences can be advantageous (such as providing opportunities and novel and interesting experiences), as well as undermine life's chances (such as discrimination, limited opportunities and diminished experiences that provide meaning to life).

A second reason to prefer the notion of *acculturative stress* is that the source of the stressful experiences lies in the interaction between cultures (hence *acculturative*), rather than in one culture or the other. Thus, by using the term *culture*, it is possible to misidentify the root of the difficulty as being in one single culture or another. True, it may sometimes lie in the dominant culture (e.g., when there is often prejudice and discrimination) or in the non-dominant culture (e.g., when there is a lack of resources, such as education or leadership, to adapt to the new situation). However, even in these examples, a case can be made that prejudice and resource shortage are essentially problems that are located in the interaction between the two cultures, rather than uniquely in one or the other. Thus, for these two reasons, the term *acculturative stress* is preferred to *culture shock*.

3.3 Acculturation Strategies

Perhaps the most frequent topic of research in the current acculturation literature is acculturation strategies. Since not everyone seeks to acculturate in the same way, it is important to conceptualize differing ways of acculturating (Padilla, 1980). The concept of acculturation strategies refers to the *how* of acculturation. Acculturation strategies consist of two components: attitudes and behaviours (that is, the preferences for, and actual practices of, ways of relating to one's own and to other groups). Of course, there is rarely a one-to-one match between what an individual prefers and seeks (attitudes) and what one is actually able to do (behaviours). This discrepancy is widely studied in social psychology and is usually explained as the result of social constraints on behaviours (such as norms, opportunities etc.). In the case of acculturation strategies, these constraints lie in the social and intercultural contexts in which an individual lives, often due to differential power of groups to pursue their preferred way of acculturating. Nevertheless, there is often a positive correlation between acculturation attitudes and actual behaviours, permitting the use of an overall assessment of individual acculturation strategies.

The centrality of the concept of acculturation strategies can be illustrated by reference to each component of the general acculturation framework (Figure 3.1). At the cultural level, the two groups in contact (whether dominant or non-dominant) usually have some notion about what they are attempting to do (e.g., colonial policies, or motivations for migration), or what is being done to them during the contact such as enslavement or discrimination. Similarly, the social, cultural and political goals of the emergent ethnocultural groups will influence their acculturation strategies. At the individual level, both the behavioural changes and acculturative stress phenomena are now known to be a function, at least to some extent, of what people try to do during their acculturation; the longer term outcomes (psychological, sociocultural and intercultural adaptations) usually have some correspondence with the strategic goals set by the groups of which they are members.

As we have seen, the original definitions of acculturation foresaw that cultural and psychological homogenization (later identified with assimilation and globalization) would not be the only possible or inevitable outcome of intercultural contact. This is because people hold different views about how they want to live following contact: not everyone seeks out such contact, and even among those who do, not everyone seeks to change their culture and behaviour to be more like the other (often dominant) group. Globalization is a journey, not a destination.

In their 1936 statement on acculturation, Redfield, Linton and Herskovits noted that assimilation is not the only form of acculturation; there are other ways of going about it. Taking this assertion as a starting point, Berry (1970; Sommerlad & Berry, 1970) first distinguished between the strategies of assimilation and integration, and later between them and separation and marginalization as alternative ways in which acculturation (both of groups and of individuals) could take place. The starting point of these distinctions was an event that occurred when I was teaching a class on racism in 1967 at the Free University of Sydney (a counter-culture social action group). This class was made up of mainly Aboriginal students who wanted to know more about academic ideas and research about racism. During the day of one of these classes, the prime minister of Australia announced a policy change with respect to relations between Aboriginal Peoples and the larger Australian society. He proposed that 'Aboriginal Peoples would become Australian like all other Australians'. Students in the class were taken aback by this announcement, and decided that this was such an important issue that consultations with

Aboriginal Peoples should be undertaken before the implementation of any such policy. The class wrote a letter to the prime minister suggesting that research was needed to discover the views of Aboriginal Peoples about 'how they wanted to relate to the rest of Australian society'. After many months, a reply was received, stating that this was a very complex issue, and that Aboriginal Peoples could not possibly understand or express a view on this issue!

In the interval, such a research project was carried out in a few Aboriginal communities by members of the class. The main finding was that two fundamental issues were of concern to Aboriginal Peoples: the maintenance and transmission of Aboriginal cultures and identities, and the degree of contact and participation with the larger Australian society desired by Aboriginal Peoples. These two issues became the foundation of the acculturation strategies framework, which has been used up until the present time. These two issues (more generally seen as the orientation towards one's own group, and orientations towards other groups in the larger society) were supplemented by a third issue: the power of individuals and groups to choose and pursue their own preferences with respect to these two orientations (Berry, 1974a, 1980a).

While the first dimension is clearly focused on one's own group, it is important to note that the second dimension (contact with others outside one's own ethnocultural group) can have many referents. In societies with a clear dominant ('mainstream') culture, it refers to this one well-established way of living in the society. However, in societies without such a mainstream, or those with very diverse cultural populations, the other groups can be ethnocultural groups that exist in the neighbourhood or in the larger society more generally. In the latter case, the contact dimension becomes more complex. As noted by van Oudenhoven and Ward (2013), these new complexities have required more refined conceptualization of who the 'others' are in the acculturation process. This complexity can be illustrated by a study with Cree indigenous peoples in northern Quebec (Berry, Wintrob, Sindell & Mawhinney, 1982). Two dominant group options were available to the Cree: the English- and French-speaking groups in their territory and in Quebec society more generally.

In the acculturation strategies framework, orientations to these issues are rendered as a relative preference for: *cultural continuity* (Issue 1: maintaining one's heritage culture and identity); *contact and participation* (Issue 2: a relative preference for having contact with and participating in the larger society along with other ethnocultural groups); and *power* (Issue 3: the relative power to choose how to pursue these two orientations). I (1974a, 1980b) developed the first strategies framework, and subsequently elaborated it. It was published in a

Scheme of Modes of Group Relations in Complex Societies Based upon Answers to Three Questions

QUESTION 1	QUESTION 2	QUESTION 3	PATTERN	
Retention of Identity?	Positive Relations?	Choice by Ethnic Group?	Number	Name
"YES"	"YES"	"YES"	1	Integration (Democratic Pluralism)
		"NO"	2	Paternal Integration (Inclusive segregation)
	"NO"	"YES"	3	Rejection (Self-segregation)
		"NO"	4	Exclusive (Segregation)
"NO"	"YES"	"YES"	5	Assimilation 1 (Melting pot)
		"NO"	6	Assimilation 2 (Pressure cooker)
	"NO"	"YES"	7	Marginality
		"NO"	8	Deculturation

Figure 3.2 Modes of acculturation in ethnocultural groups (Berry, 1980a)

volume (Padilla, 1980) based on a symposium that sought to challenge acculturation researchers to move away from a unidimensional approach to acculturation. This unidimensional approach assumed that acculturation was a linear and unidirectional process in which individuals inevitably moved away from their heritage culture towards assimilation into the dominant culture. This version (Berry, 1980a) is shown in Figure 3.2, where the strategies were called Modes of Acculturation (or Relational Attitudes).

In these early versions of the framework (Berry, 1974a, 1980a), orientations to the three issues are shown as dichotomous 'yes' or 'no' options, giving rise to eight different ways of acculturating. This early construction encouraged the notion of 'Berry Boxes' (Ward, 2008). Although I never viewed them as dichotomous choices, I (1997b, 2001) later emphasized the use of continuous dimensions, and placed the options in circles. This was an attempt to avoid individuals being 'boxed in', and to provide a more nuanced approach.

The current version (Berry, 2001) of the framework is shown in Figure 3.3, using the concept of acculturation *strategies*. The term *strategies* is used because these various ways of acculturating are not just passive responses to

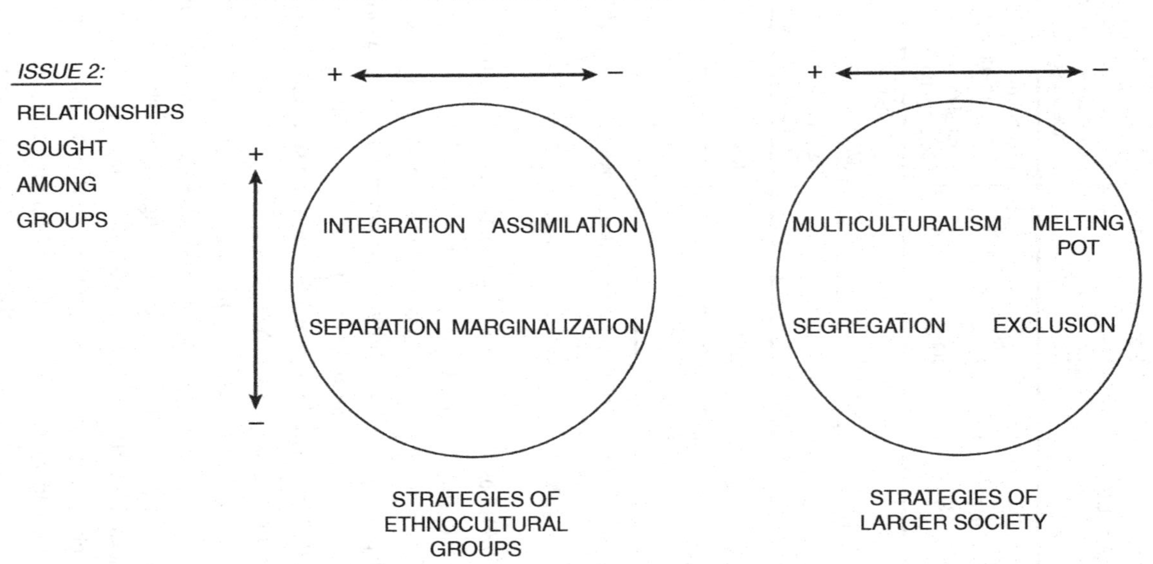

Figure 3.3 Acculturation strategies in ethnocultural groups and the larger society (Berry, 2003)

daily events and the larger intercultural context, or merely attitudinal preferences, but are consciously chosen in order to achieve a particular goal.

As noted earlier, my interest in acculturation strategies as a way of understanding variations in acculturation came about by an incident in Australia in 1967, when the prime minister announced a policy of assimilation for Aboriginal Peoples. The first studies using an early version of the acculturation strategies framework were published (Berry, 1970; Sommerlad & Berry, 1970). The subsequent elaborations were published in 1974 and 1980. Originally, these strategies were termed 'relational attitudes' because they asked about people's preferred ways to relate to their own group and to the larger society. Later, they were termed 'acculturation attitudes' (Berry, Kim, Power, Young & Bujaki, 1989), and finally 'acculturation strategies' (Berry, 2001). The notion of 'strategies' was adopted because individuals often indicated in ethnographic interviews that they were goal-seeking, attempting to achieve a particular way of engaging in their intercultural relations.

In these original frameworks, we find the conceptual basis for most subsequent conceptual and empirical work on how acculturation may take place. These early versions showed the complex interrelationships among the three issues, in which the views of the non-dominant and dominant groups interact to promote or constrain the ways in which all groups acculturate. Later frameworks, such as the Interactive Acculturation Model (Bourhis, Moïse, Perrault & Sénécal, 1997), further developed this interactive and mutual approach. Research using these models has shown that the preferred acculturation strategies differ according to which aspect of life is being examined (such as work, social relations, food, dress and family life) (Navas et al., 2005; Safdar et al., 2013). Often, there is more acceptance of assimilation in the domains of work, but a preference for integration in the domains of social relations, food and dress, and of separation with respect to family and community life.

The original conception focuses on cultural maintenance as the first issue, and intercultural contact and relationships as the second. Liebkind (2001) noted that other researchers sometimes changed the *social* focus of the second issue (contact), and replaced it with either *identification* with the larger society, or *adopting* the culture of the larger society (rather than having relationships with it). Many variations in conceptualizing this second issue have been examined empirically (e.g., Berry & Sabatier, 2011; Snauwaert, Soenens, Vanbeselaere & Boen, 2003). These studies found that varying the focus of the second issue led to variations in the frequency of those who could be considered as integrated, assimilated, separated or marginalized.

Returning to Figure 3.3, in the acculturation strategies framework, orientations to the two basic issues are seen as varying along dimensions, represented by bipolar arrows (at the top, and on the left). These strategies carry different names, depending on which group (the non-dominant or the dominant) is being considered. The strategies of the non-dominant ethnocultural groups are shown on the left; those of the larger society are shown on the right.

From the point of view of non-dominant ethnocultural groups, when individuals do not wish or are not able to maintain their cultural identity and seek daily interaction with other cultures, the *assimilation* strategy is defined. In contrast, when individuals place a value on holding on to their original culture, and at the same time wish to avoid interaction with others, then the *separation* alternative is defined. When there is an interest in both maintaining one's original culture and having daily interactions with other groups, *integration* is the option; here, there is some degree of cultural integrity maintained, while at the same time the individual seeks, as a member of an ethnocultural group, to participate as an integral part of the larger social network. Finally, when there is little possibility of or interest in cultural maintenance (often for reasons of enforced cultural loss) and little interest in having relations with others (often for reasons of exclusion or discrimination), then *marginalization* is defined.

Of course, non-dominant groups and their individual members do not always have the freedom to choose how they want to engage in intercultural relations and acculturation. Constraints imposed by the dominant group may enforce certain kinds of relations or limit the choices of non-dominant groups or individuals. This is most clearly so in the case of integration, which can only be freely chosen and successfully pursued by non-dominant groups when the dominant society is open and inclusive in its orientation towards cultural diversity (Berry, 1980a). Thus, a mutual accommodation is required for integration to be attained, involving the acceptance by both dominant and non-dominant groups of the right of all groups to live as cultural communities within the same larger society. This strategy requires non-dominant groups to accept the basic laws and norms of the larger society (such as Charters of Rights and Freedoms), while at the same time maintaining the values and interests of their own group within such a framework. As a counterpart to this acceptance, the dominant group must be prepared to adapt national institutions (e.g., education, health, labour) to better meet the needs of all groups now living together in the plural society.

The integration strategy can only be pursued by non-dominant groups and individuals in societies where certain psychological pre-conditions are established (Berry & Kalin, 1995). These pre-conditions are: the widespread acceptance of the value to a society of cultural diversity (i.e., the presence of a positive multicultural ideology); relatively low levels of prejudice (i.e., minimal ethnocentrism, racism and discrimination); positive mutual attitudes among all ethnocultural groups (i.e., no specific intergroup hatreds); and a sense of attachment to or identification with the larger society by all individuals and groups. Moreover, integration (and separation) can only be pursued when other members of one's ethnocultural group share in the wish to maintain the group's cultural heritage and identity. In this sense, these two strategies are 'collectivistic', whereas assimilation is more 'individualistic' (Lalonde & Cameron, 1993; Moghaddam, 1988). When these strategies are assessed using separate scales, it is possible to observe variable degrees of preference for each strategy independently. For example, one could logically have a positive orientation towards both integration and separation, since both strategies involve a preference for the maintenance of one's cultural heritage and identity.

In the right-hand circle of Figure 3.3 are the strategies that may exist in the larger society. These strategies have been referred to as the *acculturation expectations* (Berry, 2003) held by members of the larger society. These expectations may be manifested in public attitudes and policies regarding how dominant people think that non-dominant groups and individuals *should* acculturate; they also include views about how dominant members of the larger society should themselves acculturate. The terms in this circle are widely used. Assimilation, when sought by the dominant group, is termed the *melting pot.* When separation is demanded and enforced by the dominant group, it is *segregation*. Marginalization, when imposed by the dominant group, is a form of *exclusion*. Finally, integration, when cultural diversity is an objective of the larger society as a whole, and is widely accepted by its members, represents the strategy of mutual accommodation now widely called *multiculturalism*.

The original definition of acculturation identified it as a *mutual* process. To understand this mutual character of acculturation, it is necessary to examine the acculturation strategies and policies of members both of ethnocultural groups and of the larger society. To accomplish this, research in Canada (Berry & Kalin, 1995; Berry, Kalin & Taylor, 1977) has employed a scale (termed *multicultural ideology*) in national surveys. This scale represents items supporting integration at its positive pole, and items supporting the other three strategies at its negative pole. Since the early 1980s, support for multiculturalism in Canada (as indicated by scores on the multicultural ideology scale) has risen from about 65 per cent to about 70 per cent (Berry, 2013a).

As noted earlier, conceptualizations of these acculturation strategies have become more complex in recent years. For example, Bourhis and colleagues (1997) have carried out a series of studies using an 'interactive acculturation model' that examines attitudes of both groups in contact. They find individual differences in these preferences, and, most importantly, differences between the non-dominant and dominant groups studied. Not only are there more groups with which to be in contact (van Oudenhoven & Ward, 2012), the domains of life that are subject to change have been elaborated (Navas et al., 2005; Safdar et al., 2012). These studies have shown that the preferred acculturation strategies differ according to which aspect of life is being examined (such as work, social relations, food, dress and family life). Often, there is more acceptance of assimilation in the domains of work, but a preference for integration in the domains of social relations, food and dress, and of separation with respect to family and community life.

4 Adaptation to Acculturation

Finally (on the right of Figure 3.1), the longer-term outcomes of acculturation are shown as three forms of adaptation to acculturation. This concept refers to *how well* individuals succeed in daily life in their own group and in the larger society. Originally, two kinds of adaptations were identified (Ward, 2001). First are adaptations that are primarily internal or *psychological* (e.g., a sense of wellbeing, or self-esteem, sometimes called 'feeling well'). Second are *sociocultural* adaptations (sometimes called 'doing well'). These adaptations link the individual to others in the new society, and are manifested for example by competence in the activities of daily intercultural living, including social relations and success at school and work and in community life. A third form of adaptation has come to the fore in recent years: *intercultural* adaptation (Berry, 2015, 2017). Here, the interest is in how well individuals manage to achieve workable relationships with others across cultural boundaries within the plural society (essentially 'relating well'). The focus here is on the achievement of positive intercultural relationships (such as mutually positive ethnic group attitudes, and a lack of prejudice and discrimination), and the acceptance of a multicultural ideology, which as noted earlier is a general view that places a value on both cultural diversity and equitable participation by everyone in the larger society.

All these forms of adaptation are relevant to members of both the non-dominant ethnocultural groups and the larger society. They all feed into an individual's overall wellbeing. If they are successful, individuals will have a coherent and positive sense of self, supportive social interactions and networks and congenial intercultural relationships. If not successful, individuals will have low self-esteem, feelings of incompetence in daily life in the community and hostile relationships with other cultural communities in the larger society.

4.1 Psychological Adaptation

In more detail, psychological adaptation is conceptualized and assessed by notions and measures that are linked to the acculturation process, particularly with the experience of acculturative stress (Berry, 2006a). It is this form of adaptation that comes closest to concerns about personal health and wellbeing. On the positive side, psychological adaptation includes concepts and measures that assess subjective wellbeing, self-esteem and achieving a consolidated identity while living interculturally. This form of adaptation is equally relevant to both non-dominant and dominant communities during the process of their mutual acculturation.

4.2 Sociocultural Adaptation

This form of adaptation refers, on the positive side, to the development, learning and achievement of competence in the tasks of daily intercultural living (Masgoret & Ward, 2006). When dealing with two cultures, individuals need to know the basic rules, norms and ways of dealing with officials, institutions and technologies. These skills all take time to develop, and are enabled by a process of social learning. On the negative side, problems such as deviant social behaviour (e.g., gangs), personal behaviours (e.g., addictions) and a lack of institutional involvement (e.g., unemployment, truancy) are all indicators.

4.3 Intercultural Adaptation

Intercultural adaptation refers, on the negative side, to having prejudice and hostile attitudes towards ethnocultural groups, engaging in discrimination and rejecting the value of cultural diversity and equal participation in one's plural society. On the positive side, intercultural adaptation refers to being minimally prejudiced, not engaging in acts of discrimination, having mutually positive attitudes towards various ethnocultural groups and accepting an ideology of multiculturalism.

4.4 Three Hypotheses

In order to understand the origins of these three forms of adaptation, I (2017) have advanced three hypotheses: integration, multiculturalism and contact.

4.4.1 Integration Hypothesis

The integration hypothesis (Berry, 1997b) proposes that when individuals and groups are 'doubly engaged' (in both their heritage cultures and in the life of the larger society) by adopting the integration strategy, they will be more successful in their lives, including having a sense of personal wellbeing, developing sociocultural competence and having positive intercultural relations. In much research on acculturation, the integration strategy has been found to lead to better adaptation than other strategies (Berry, 1997b). Berry, Phinney, Sam and Vedder (2006a, 2006b) in an international study of immigrant youth, found that those who were pursuing the integration strategy had better psychological and sociocultural adaptation. Nguyen and Benet-Martínez (2013) carried out a meta-analysis across 83 studies and more than 20,000 participants; they concluded that integration is associated with better adaptation. Specifically, they found that integration ('biculturalism' in their terms) has a significant and positive relationship with both psychological adaptation (e.g., life satisfaction, positive affect, self-esteem) and sociocultural adaptation (e.g., academic achievement, career success, social skills, lack of behavioural problems). A further analysis of the data set from a study of immigrant youth (Berry et al., 2006a, 2006b) by Abu-Rayya and Sam (2017) confirmed this relationship between integration and wellbeing. A possible explanation for this relationship between integration and these positive outcomes is that those who are 'doubly engaged' with both cultures receive support and resources from both, and are competent in dealing with both. The social capital afforded by these multiple social and cultural engagements may well offer the route to success in plural societies.

4.4.2 Multiculturalism Hypothesis

The multiculturalism hypothesis proposes that when people feel secure in their own cultures, they will be in a position to accept those who differ from themselves. This hypothesis was derived from a statement in the Canadian multiculturalism policy (Government of Canada, 1971) that when individuals feel secure as members of their cultural communities, this will provide the psychological basis for more positive intercultural relations (including a willingness for intercultural contact, respect for others and the reduction of discrimination). For many years, my colleagues and I (Berry et al., 1977) have studied the central role of perceived security in the acceptance of others in plural societies. We have proposed three aspects of security: *cultural, economic and personal* (Berry & Kalin, 2000). Cultural security refers to the feeling that one's cultural values, traditions, norms, language and other ethnocultural traits are accepted in the larger society. Economic security refers to the sense that the socioeconomic position of oneself and one's group will remain intact despite the presence of cultural others. Finally, personal security includes the feeling that oneself and one's family is not in any personal danger from cultural others. These three forms of security are considered a psychological prerequisite for positive intercultural relations in all groups (both dominant and non-dominant) in contact (Berry et al., 1977). There is now substantial empirical evidence to support the multiculturalism hypothesis in various countries (Berry, 2017; Berry & Kalin, 2000; Berry et al., 1977; Kruusvall, Vetik & Berry, 2009; Lebedeva & Tatarko, 2013; Ward & Masgoret, 2008).

Since the introduction of the multiculturalism hypothesis in 1977, the relationship has been proposed in an inverse way (called the 'integrated threat hypothesis') by Stephan and colleagues (Stephan, Renfro, Esses, Stephan & Martin, 2005). They proposed that a sense of threat will undermine the possibility of engaging in positive intercultural relations. The threat hypothesis argues that a sense of threat to a person's identity will lead to rejection of the group that is the source of threat. In short, the development of intercultural adaptation is supported by a sense of security and confidence, and undermined by threats, whether symbolic (cultural) or material (economic).

4.4.3 Contact Hypothesis

The contact hypothesis proposes that intercultural contact and sharing will promote mutual acceptance under certain conditions, especially that of equality between the groups (Allport, 1954). In national surveys in Canada, Kalin and Berry (1982) found substantial support for this relationship, especially when status is controlled. Pettigrew and Tropp (2011) carried out meta-analyses of numerous studies of the contact hypothesis, which came from many countries and many diverse settings (such as schools, work and experiments). Their findings provide general support for the contact hypothesis: intergroup contact does generally relate negatively to prejudice in both dominant and non-dominant samples. Contact appears to promote intercultural adaptation.

5 Assessment of Acculturation and Adaptation

All aspects of the acculturation framework (Figure 3.1) require assessment in order to understand each component and their empirical interrelationships. These assessment procedures have been described a number of times, and are only outlined here (Berry, Trimble et al., 1986; van de Vijver, Celenk & Berry, 2016).

5.1 Cultures in Contact

First, for the dominant culture, some key features brought to the contact setting need to be assessed. These include the purpose, length, permanence, numbers, policies and some cultural qualities that are brought to the contact arena, such as guns, medicines, seeds, ploughs and the political organization that is imposed. For the non-dominant culture, similar features need to be assessed; in this case, the details needing to be understood are quite different, including habitat destruction and political organization to resist occupation and domination. Second, the changes in both cultures need examination, including their languages, religions, social organization and economic organization. Together these set the stage for the assessment of psychological acculturation and adaptation.

The degree to which individuals are exposed to and participate in these cultural changes also requires assessment. Simply being in a culture-contact setting does not mean that individuals will actually engage with members of other cultural groups. Neither is length of time in the contact setting a useful proxy for such exposure. This engagement has been termed *contact acculturation* (Berry, 1976; Berry, van de Koppel et al., 1986) and is assessed by interviews with individuals and observations of their lifestyle. Two points arise in this regard: first, it is not possible to refer to one 'degree' or 'level' of acculturation (e.g., as in 'highly acculturated'), but only to the level of support for each of the four acculturation strategies. When 'level of acculturation' is used in the literature, it is often intended to mean 'level of assimilation' only. Second, however, if one is referring to length or frequency of contact with, or to the degree of participation in the larger society, then the notion of 'level' is appropriate to refer to the degree of involvement in the larger society. However, this usage says nothing about heritage cultural maintenance. This actual degree of contact and engagement is a kind of 'independent variable' in acculturation research, and provides an estimate of the *potential* for change during psychological acculturation.

In my early research, I made a simple division between 'traditional' and 'transitional' community samples (Berry, 1966b, 1971, 1976) as a rough indicator of the degree of prior contact. Evidence for making this distinction between samples was based on the history of contact and on observations of the degree to which the communities appeared to have remained much as they were in earlier ethnographic accounts, or had moved away moved from these earlier ways of living. Then, to obtain some validation of these average community differences, and to assess individual differences in contact acculturation, individuals were asked questions about their experience of schooling, wage employment, ownership of various introduced items (such as radios or washing machines) and travel outside their communities. These variables have been used frequently in subsequent research to estimate the degree of an individual's actual exposure to another culture (Berry et al., 2006a and 2006b; Berry, van de Koppel et al., 1986; Mishra & Berry, 2017; Mishra et al., 1996).

5.2 Psychological Acculturation

The degree to which individuals change their behaviours (*psychological acculturation* in the middle of Figure 3.1) as a result of such intercultural contact is assessed by noting their *behavioural changes* and their experience of *acculturative stress*. These changes also include the development of *acculturation strategies* that individuals employ during their experience of intercultural contact (as described in Figures 3.2 and 3.3).

5.2.1 Behavioural Changes

The degree to which individuals have been able to establish a new way of living during and following their acculturation experiences has been termed *adaptation*, and includes *psychological, sociocultural* and *intercultural* forms (as shown on the right of Figure 3.2).

There is a vast research literature on the kind and degree of behavioural change following culture contact. These include studies of changes in social relationships (with an individual's own group and with other groups), in cultural identities (own group and national society) and in languages known and spoken (own and national). This literature is too vast to present here, but may be sampled by examining recent handbooks (e.g., Sam & Berry, 2006/2016; Schwartz & Unger, 2017).

More complex behavioural changes are also examined, including work and academic activities. In many of these cases, standard tests have been used, with only slight modifications to the test instructions and language. Assessment of these complex behavioural changes has usually started with the concepts and measures already available in WASP, and taken to the sample as an *imposed etic* (Berry, 1969, 1989). Modifications to these concepts and measures sometimes pass through an *emic* examination of the indigenous meanings and behavioural expressions in a particular culture. For example, with respect to cognitive style, on the assumption that the process of disembedding is a psychological universal, a tool for assessing it in India (the Story Pictorial Embedded Figures Test) was created by Sinha (1978) to elicit responses. A later modification (the African Embedded Figures Test) was developed by Berry et al. (1986). In both cases, local objects were used in the drawings presented to participants. However, sometimes the original tools (with changes in only language, instructions and training) have been used (e.g., Berry, 1976). In such cases, the usual cautions about equivalence and comparability need to be observed (Berry, 1969; Van de Vijver & Leung, 1997). In these cases, there is usually a search for a relationship between an estimate of contact acculturation (length and intensity of contact) and acculturation strategies and these behavioural changes.

5.2.2 Acculturative Stress

Despite the earlier comments on stress being both positive and negative in valence, assessment of acculturative stress has often emphasized the negative aspects of being challenged by intercultural contact. Cawte (1972) developed a scale that has three domains. First is anxiety, which is often considered a result of general feelings of uncertainty; during acculturation, this uncertainty arises from not knowing how to feel and behave in the two or more cultures. Second, depression is usually associated with a sense of loss; during acculturation, there is frequently a sense of loss (and often a real loss) of contact with and support from a person's heritage culture. Third, psychosomatic symptoms often accompany changes in social and physical settings; during acculturation, these include disruptions to digestion and sleep. This scale has been used in many subsequent studies (e.g., Berry, 1976; Berry et al., 2006a, 2006b), and is similar to other measures used (e.g., by Safdar et al., 2012).

Some other conceptualizations and measures of acculturative stress have been developed (Benet-Martínez & Haritatos, 2005; Mena, Padilla & Maldonado, 1987; Rodriguez, Myers, Mira, Flores & Garcia-Hernandez, 2002). However, they focus more on the source of the stress (the *stressors*) such as work challenges, language difficulties, discrimination and social isolation rather than the outcome.

5.2.3 Acculturation Strategies

Acculturation strategies have been assessed in many ways. The first was to consider the four strategies as distinct ways to acculturate, and to create four scales to assess each one (Berry, 1976; Berry et al., 1989). The second was to consider the two underlying issues as distinct and to create two scales, one to asses each dimension (Dona & Berry, 1994). The third has been to create four vignettes, one to capture the core meaning of each strategy (Pruegger, 1993). The fourth was to assess a number of intercultural variables and to create acculturation profiles based on profile analysis (Berry et al., 2006a, 2006b).

For all these approaches, ethnographic work is needed to capture the domains of intercultural interaction about which acculturating individuals may have preferences, such as food, dress, identity, language, social relations, media use and gender relations.

For the first method, items expressing the four strategies in each domain are created. These items are assessed in pilot work for their face validity, and then administered to a preliminary sample to obtain data on item–item and item–total correlations and Cronbach alpha for each of the four scales. Validation is carried out using the 'known group' method where members of particular groups are expected to score in particular ways (high or low) on each scale. For example, individuals who read both ethnic and national newspapers should score higher on the integration scale than those who read only national (assimilation high), ethnic (separation high) or no newspapers (marginalization high). The four scales are responded to on Likert-type response scales, and total scores on each of the four scales assigned to each respondent. An example of a set of items (Ataca, 1998) is:

I. I would like my children to learn both Turkish and Canadian values and customs.
A. I would like my children to learn Canadian values and customs more than Turkish values and customs.
M. I don't really care whether my children learn any values or customs.
S. I would like my children to learn Turkish values and customs more than Canadian values and customs.

For the second method, the same first steps are followed to create items that represent preferences for the two underlying issues (cultural/identity maintenance and contact/participation) rather than for the four specific strategies. Total scores are created for each dimension, and then can either be 'crossed' to create scores for the four strategies or used as scores on the two dimensions. Items are (Dona, 1990):

Cultural maintenance. I want my children to go to Latin American heritage classes.
Participation. I want my children to join in Canadian customs.

One issue frequently discussed in the research literature is how to cross the scores on these two dimensions by splitting the distribution to create the four strategies. The first study (Dona & Berry, 1994) split scores on the dimensions at the median, such that half the respondents are above and half are below this cut point. Others have used the mean score, or the theoretical midpoint (e.g., 3 on a five-point scale). Debates have raised the issue of the 'best' way to make the cut (Berry & Sabatier, 2011; Snauwaert et al., 2003) but so far, no one way has proven generally superior.

The third method develops vignettes that capture the essence of the four strategies (Pruegger, 1993). These are developed via the same ethnographic approach used in the first two methods. Respondents are asked to either rank them in order of their preference or to assign a score on a Likert scale.

I. I am very proud of my culture and traditions. I think it is very important to keep them alive and respect the ways of our ancestors. However, I feel it is equally important to maintain good relations with non-Aboriginal peoples. I believe that we have much to offer each other. It is important to me to preserve my own cultural heritage while actively participating in Anglo-Canadian society.

A. I am very proud of my culture and its traditions. But I think Aboriginal peoples do themselves great harm by trying to keep them alive and hang onto the ways of our elders. In order to be accepted and move ahead in today's world it is necessary for us to establish good relations with non-Aboriginal peoples by adopting the attitudes and behaviours of other Canadians. Only by rejecting our past and actively participating in Anglo-Canadian society will we be able to fit in and survive as equals in Canada.

M. I do not really understand the culture and traditions of my people. Because of this, I do not feel that I fit into the Aboriginal community. Nor do I feel comfortable in the non-Aboriginal community. They make me feel different, like an outsider. I just don't feel like I belong anywhere.

S. I am very proud of my culture and its traditions. I think it is very important to keep them alive and respect the ways of our ancestors. The only way to do this is to have as little contact with non-Aboriginal peoples as possible. I think Aboriginal peoples should stick to ourselves and have very little contact with Anglo-Canadian society.

The fourth approach has been to create *acculturation profiles*, combining statements (similar to those just presented) with other indicators, such as cultural identities, social relationships and language use. These are usually presented on two dimensions (ethnic and national orientations). My colleagues and I (2006a, 2006b) used these profiles in our study of immigrant youth, and Abu-Rayya and Sam (2017) used them to obtain a more comprehensive picture with multiple variables assessing acculturation preferences and behaviours.

5.3 Adaptation

The degree to which individuals have been able to establish a new way of living during and following acculturation experiences has been termed *adaptation*, and includes psychological, sociocultural and intercultural forms (as shown on the right of Figure 3.2). These three forms of adaptation have been dubbed *feeling well, doing well* and *relating well*.

5.3.1 Psychological Adaptation

Psychological adaptation has been assessed in various ways. The most common is to use a number of indicators of personal wellbeing, such as self-esteem, life satisfaction and mental health (e.g., Berry et al., 2006a, 2006b; Berry & Hou, 2016, 2017). If these measures reveal positive intercorrelations, they are sometimes combined into a single index to provide a more comprehensive estimate. Psychological adaptation is usually measured in both the non-dominant and dominant groups in order to provide an estimate of how well the various groups are adapting.

Self-esteem has items that assess the degree to which an individual feels good about themselves in general, but is not specifically related to acculturation. Sample items are: 'On the whole, I am satisfied with myself.' (+), and 'At times, I think I am no good at all.' (−)

Life satisfaction has items that assess the degree to which individuals feel that they have achieved a satisfactory life. As for self-esteem, life satisfaction is not specifically related to acculturation. Sample items are: 'In most ways, my life is close to my ideal.' (+), and 'I am satisfied with my life.' (+)

Mental health is sometimes assessed with a single very general item: 'In general, would you say your mental health is excellent, very good, good, fair, or poor?' (e.g., Berry & Hou, 2016).

5.3.2 Sociocultural Adaptation

Sociocultural adaptation was originally assessed using a scale of problems being experienced in the new society. This scale has items that are specifically related to the difficult experiences during acculturation, rather than to more positive indicators, resulting in a score that was in a negative direction (i.e., a high score meaning poor sociocultural adaptation). Recently, Wilson, Ward, Velichko and Bethel (2017) have produced a revised sociocultural adaptation scale that has a high score indicating positive sociocultural adaptation. Items include competence in such domains as: building and maintaining relationships, obtaining community services, understanding and speaking the host society language of the society of settlement and interacting at social events.

This form of adaptation is usually only examined in the non-dominant groups. However, adaptation to daily intercultural living is also a challenge for the dominant group and in principle can be assessed among its members as well (Haugen & Kunst, 2017).

5.3.3 Intercultural Adaptation

I (2015) introduced the concept of intercultural adaptation as an indicator of how well individuals are dealing with others in the new society, even though these issues had been part of acculturation research for decades. The concept includes Multicultural Ideology and Tolerance. This first concept assesses the degree to which individuals accept that cultural diversity and inclusiveness are good for a society and for oneself. It is usually assessed in both the non-dominant and dominant communities in a plural society.

Multicultural Ideology (Berry et al., 1977) includes items such as: 'We should recognize that cultural and racial diversity is a fundamental characteristic of [national] society.' (+); and 'If people of different ethnic and cultural origins want to keep their own culture, they should keep it to themselves.' (−). Tolerance includes items such as: 'Immigrants should have as much say about the future of this country as people who were born and raised here.' (+); and 'It is a bad idea for people of different races/ethnicities to marry one another.' (−).

Taken together, these three forms of adaptation can provide an indication of how well acculturating individuals are adapting to each other in their new lives.

With these conceptual and methodological issues behind us, I now turn to a brief survey of my research around the world.

6 Empirical Research on Acculturation around the World

In this section, my focus is on two distinct kinds of groups: Indigenous Peoples, and Immigrants, Refugees and Ethnocultural Groups. I make no attempt to provide a comprehensive account of my work, or of the work of others. The various handbooks of acculturation (Chun, Balls-Organista & Marin, 2003; Sam & Berry, 2006, 2016; Schwartz & Unger, 2017) are excellent sources to obtain a more comprehensive picture of acculturation.

As noted in the introduction, my research work on acculturation is rooted in my own personal experiences in early life. In this work, my perspective and approach are rooted in multicultural Canadian society (which serves as my 'larger society'), and much of the rest of the world ('ethnocultural communities'). This background has necessarily tilted my conceptualizations, assessments and interpretations in a particular direction.

Some basic principles have served to guide this work, all emphasizing three kinds of comparison. I have been sampling: (i) across kinds of acculturating groups; (ii) across societies of settlement; and (iii) between non-dominant and dominant peoples living in these various societies. Two frameworks have helped me to structure this sampling and these comparisons.

First is the need to understand the sociopolitical roots of acculturating peoples living in plural societies. The first of these frameworks (see Figure 6.1, from Berry, 2006b) shows the kinds of acculturating groups living in culturally plural societies, and organizes them according to three dimensions: voluntariness, mobility and permanence. Comparisons can be made across

MOBILITY	VOLUNTARINESS OF CONTACT	
	VOLUNTARY	INVOLUNTARY
SEDENTARY	ETHNOCULTURAL GROUPS	INDIGENOUS PEOPLES
MIGRANT Permanent temporary	IMMIGRANTS SOJOURNERS	REFUGEES ASYLUM SEEKERS

Figure 6.1 Types of groups in plural societies

these dimensions to examine whether these three factors provide differential contexts for understanding their acculturation.

One way to conceive of this variety of groups is by looking at the reasons (historical or contemporary) for people of different cultural backgrounds to live together. First, groups may find themselves together either because they have sought out such an arrangement *voluntarily* or because it has been forced upon them. Second, some groups have remained on home ground, while others have settled far from their ancestral territory (*sedentary vs migrant*). And third, some people are settled into a plural society *permanently*, while others are settled only *temporarily*.

Some of the more common terms used to refer to constituent groups in plural societies have been placed in Figure 6.1 in relation to these three dimensions. Starting with the longest-term and sedentary residents, *Indigenous Peoples* are those who have 'always been there' in the sense that their roots go way back, and there is little evidence of any earlier people whose descendants are still in the population of the society. The basic characteristic of many Indigenous Peoples is that their territories have been forcefully incorporated into a larger nation-state, their residual lands are often reduced in size and capacity to sustain life and they have come to be seen as just another 'minority' group within the larger plural society, rather than having indigenous rights. They are clearly involuntary, as well as sedentary. These groups are sometimes referred to as 'the Fourth World', and include cultural groups such as the Inuit and Sami in the Circumpolar region, Aborigines in Australia and Adivasi in India.

Other peoples who have a long history of settlement and who are sedentary are the descendants of earlier waves of immigrants who have settled into recognizable groups, often with a sense of their own cultural heritage (such as a common language and identity). These *ethnocultural groups* may be large or small, powerful or powerless, depending on the overall history and the national context within which they live. Whatever their histories, most are now voluntary participants in the national life of their contemporary societies. Such groups include French-Canadians, Mexican-Americans and Japanese-Brasilians. In some countries, these groups are referred to as 'National Minorities', and include such groups as the Basque in Spain and France, the South Tyroleans in Italy, the Catalan in Spain and the Hakka in China.

In contrast to these two sedentary constituents of plural societies are other people who have developed in other places and been socialized into other cultures, and who migrate to take up residence (either permanently or temporarily) in another society. Among these groups are *immigrants* who usually move in order to achieve a better life elsewhere. For most, the 'pull factors' (those that attract them to a new society) are stronger than the 'push factors' (those that pressure them to leave). Hence, immigrants are generally thought of as voluntary members of plural societies. Such groups include, for example, Poles in Iceland and Indians and Chinese in Canada.

While immigrants are relatively permanent residents in their new society, the group known as *sojourners* is there only temporarily in a variety of roles, and for a set and limited purpose (e.g., as international students, diplomats, business executives, aid workers or guest workers). In their case, the process of becoming involved in the larger society is complicated by their knowledge that they will usually eventually leave, and either return home or be posted to yet another country. Thus, there may be a hesitation to become fully involved, to establish close relationships or to begin to identify with the new society. Despite their uncertain position, in some societies, sojourners constitute a substantial element in the resident population and may either hold substantial power or be relatively powerless. Such groups include Filipinas in Hong Kong and South Asians in the Gulf States.

Among involuntary migrants, *refugees* and *asylum seekers* (now often called collectively 'forced migrants') have the greatest hurdles to face: they frequently don't want to leave their homelands, and if they do, it is not always possible for them to be granted the right to stay and settle into the new society. Those who arrive at the border of a country that has signed the Geneva Convention on Refugees have a right to be admitted and given sanctuary (as asylum seekers) until their claim is adjudicated; if granted permanent admission as refugees, much of the uncertainty that surrounded their life during their flight is reduced. However, most live with the knowledge that 'push factors' (rather than 'pull factors') led them to flee their homeland and settle in their new society. And of course, most have experienced traumatic events, and most have lost their material possessions. Such groups include the Vietnamese fleeing the war there and Syrians and Afghanis fleeing the invasion and wars in their countries.

There are a number of reasons why the six kinds of groups portrayed in Figure 3.3 were organized according to the three factors (voluntary-involuntary, sedentary-migrant and permanent-temporary), rather than simply listed. The most important reason is that, as groups, they carry differential size, power, rights and resources; these factors have an important bearing on how they will engage (as groups or as individuals) in the acculturation process. A second important reason is that the attitudes, motives, values and abilities (all psychological characteristics of individuals in these groups) are also highly variable. These factors too impact how their acculturation is likely to take place.

SIX TYPES OF ACCULTURATING GROUP	LARGER SOCIETY			
	AUSTRALIA	BRASIL	CANADA	•••▶
1. IMMIGRANTS	IMA	IMB	IMC	•••▶
Armenians	IMAa			
Bengalis	IMAb			
Chinese	IMAc			
Danes	IMAd			
2. REFUGEES	RFA			
3. ASYLUM SEEKERS	ASA			
4. INDIGENOUS PEOPLES	IPA			
5. ETHNOCULTURAL GROUPS	EGA			
6. SOJOURNERS	SOA			

Figure 6.2 Comparison strategy for assessing acculturative stress and adaptation

This second framework (Figure 6.2) builds on the first one, and focuses specifically on the acculturative stress and the adaptations that these different types of groups are likely to experience. The figure lays out a comparative framework that lists the types of acculturating groups (down the left side) and the societies of settlement across the top. The expectation is that these three dimensions in Figure 6.1 provide a cumulative set of risk factors: sedentary, voluntary and permanent groups (ethnocultural groups) should have the lowest risk for acculturative stress and poor adaptation; in contrast, groups who migrate involuntarily and who are temporary (asylum seekers) should have the highest risk for acculturative stress and poorest adaptation. These expectations can be evaluated by making comparisons across societies of settlement as well as across types of acculturating groups (Berry et al., 1987). Some studies have been done to fill in these cells. For example, different groups of indigenous peoples can be compared within one society, such as in Canada (Berry, 1976) and India (Mishra & Berry, 2017).

The same group of immigrants may be compared across different societies of settlement (e.g., see Berry et al., 2006a, 2006b, for samples of Turkish and Vietnamese youth). That study found limited effects of the degree of diversity of a society of settlement on the psychological and sociocultural adaptation of immigrant youth. However, recent re-analysis of these data by Breton (2019) has shown that there are indeed effects of the policies of the society of settlement on the ethnic and national identities of immigrant youth. Similarly, Igarashi (2019 has examined these two identities in immigrants in a sample of European societies. He found that cultural diversity policy did relate to differential identity strength. These analyses exemplify the strategy of keeping sample type constant while varying the policy context of the society of settlement.

In this way, intercultural psychology crosses paths with cross-cultural psychology by making comparisons of intercultural interactions across groups, within societies across cultures. This double comparison is required because a single study of a single group settled in a single society cannot provide any indication of the broader validity of what is happening during the acculturation process. Multiple samples are required of both different types of non-dominant groups and of dominant groups, of differing societies of settlement. The universalist goal in acculturation research (as in the rest of cross-cultural and intercultural psychology) is to arrive at some general psychological principles that are valid for all human beings as a whole. For acculturation research specifically, we seek to identify these principles that may be operating in differing acculturating groups in differing settlement contexts.

6.1 Indigenous Peoples: Canada, Sierra Leone, Australia, New Guinea and India

My first entry into the field of acculturation research was with samples of Indigenous Peoples in Africa, Canada, Australia and New Guinea; later, I worked among Adivasi in India with colleagues. As noted earlier, the initial conception was to simply distinguish between those samples who had different experiences of interculturral contact, divided into 'traditional' and 'transitional' samples.

The selection of these samples was based on their documented acculturation history (length and permanence of European contact) and by an assessment of individual levels of Western schooling and experience of wage employment. I lived in these communities for a few months each and verified this allocation by ethnographic observations and interviews. The goal was to examine whether the behaviours of interest (their cognitive style of field dependence/independence, various perceptual and cognitive abilities and some social behaviours, such as independence/conformity) differed between these samples, as predicted by both their ecological and sociopolitical contexts. Specifically, these behaviours were expected to vary between hunter/gatherer and agricultural samples, and between the traditional and traditional samples.

The first study was with Temne in Sierra Leone and Inuit (then called 'Eskimo') in Arctic Canada. The samples came from remote villages (Mayola and Pond Inlet, respectively) and regional towns (Port Loko and Iqaluit, respectively). In New Guinea, I worked in a highland hunting/gathering region (Telefomin) and a coastal farming/fishing community (Hanuabada). Similarly, in Australia, I worked in a hunting/gathering settlement in the Simpson Desert (Arunta people in Santa Teresa) and a coastal farming/fishing community (Yarrabah). In all these studies, my interest was on the relationships between ecological and sociopolitical contexts and the development and display of some perceptual, cognitive and social behaviours. These studies were published in Berry (1966b, 1967, 1971, 1972, 1974b, 1976, 1979).

As noted earlier, my interest in acculturation strategies as a way of understanding variations in acculturation came about by an incident in Australia in 1967, when the prime minister announced a policy of assimilation for Aboriginal Peoples. The first studies using an early version of the acculturation strategies framework were published (Berry, 1970; Sommerlad & Berry, 1970). The subsequent elaborations were published in 1974 and 1980. Originally these strategies were termed 'relational attitudes' because they asked about people's preferred ways to relate to their own group and to the larger society. Later, they were termed 'acculturation attitudes' (Berry et al., 1989), and finally 'acculturation strategies' (Berry, 2001). The notion of 'strategies' was adopted because individuals often indicated in ethnographic interviews that they were goal-seeking, attempting to achieve a particular way of engaging in their intercultural relations.

Empirical studies followed these conceptual changes. The overview volume (Berry, 1976) included the studies noted earlier (Berry, 1966b, 1971), but added research with other indigenous peoples in Canada: Cree in northern Quebec, Ojibwe in northern Ontario and Dene and Tsimshian in northern British Colombia. The work with the Cree made use of the contacts I had from my time as a seaman in Hudson Bay and James Bay in 1959. Some of this work was directed towards providing evidence at an injunction hearing to stop the damming of their rivers (Richardson, 1974). We were seeking evidence for cultural and psychological difficulties related to their forced relocation, especially for increased acculturative stress and adaptation problems as a result of the construction of a hydroelectric dam on Cree territory (Berry, 1977; Berry et al., 1982).

Studies of the impact of formal schooling on the cultural identity (Berry, 1999) and cognition of Cree and Ojibwe people of northern Ontario were the focus of a programme of research carried out with anthropologist JoAnne Bennett. We investigated the use of the syllabic script, and its relationship with formal schooling in this context where literacy in this script is widespread in the absence of such schooling (Berry & Bennett, 1989). We found that performance on cognitive tasks was equal among those who were literate in the syllabic script (but who had no formal schooling) and those who had formal schooling. We concluded that the accultarative experience of formal schooling did not enhance cognitive performance beyond the advantage gained by being literate in the indigenous script.

At the request of the Cree School Board in the community of Big Trout Lake, we also sought to elucidate the indigenous meaning of competence among the Cree, and how it was being affected by European contact and formal schooling (Berry & Bennett, 1992). We found that the Cree concept of competence is centred on three notions of respect: for self, for others and for the natural environment. There was little variation in this core conceptualization that was linked to the accultarative experience of formal schooling. Cultural continuity in this important Cree concept was being maintained.

We sought to replicate and extend these earlier studies of Indigenous Peoples in Canada (Berry, 1976) with work in Central Africa (with the Biaka 'Pygmy' and the Bagandu people) and the Central African Republic. We found that the ecological context (hunting/gathering versus farming) was a factor in the development of cognitive style, but equally important was their experience of contact acculturation, through formal schooling, wage employment and urbanization.

The most recent programme of work with Indigenous Peoples has been in India in collaboration with the late Durganand Sinha and Ramesh Mishra (Mishra & Berry, 2017; Mishra et al., 1996). This was carried out with various groups of Adivasi Peoples (Birhor, Asur and Oraon) in the State of Bihar and elsewhere in India. The ecological and acculturation contexts varied across these groups from hunting/gathering to dry agriculture to irrigation agriculture to urban living. We examined their cognitive style and various cognitive abilities. Both the ecological and culture contact factors were found to be related to these cognitive performances.

6.2 Immigrants, Refugees and Ethnocultural Groups: Canada, China and Russia

My first major examination of acculturation and intercultural relations with non-indigenous peoples was carried out in Canada in the 1970s (Berry et al.,

1977). When the prime minister of Canada announced a 'Policy of Multiculturalism' in 1971, we wrote to him to suggest that this substantial change in policy (shifting from assimilation to multiculturalism) deserved full research investigation. We were funded to carry out a project with a large face-to-face representative samples of Canadians.

The core policy statement read as follows:

> A policy of multiculturalism within a bilingual framework [is] the most suitable means of assuring the cultural freedom of all Canadians. Such a policy should help to break down discriminatory attitudes and cultural jealousies. National unity, if it is to mean anything in the deeply personal sense, must be founded on confidence in one's own individual identity; out of this can grow respect for that of others, and a willingness to share ideas, attitudes and assumptions . . . The Government will support and encourage the various cultural and ethnic groups that give structure and vitality to our society. They will be encouraged to share their cultural expression and values with other Canadians and so contribute to a richer life for all. (Government of Canada, 1971)

An examination of this text reveals three main components to this policy. The first component is the goal of the policy, which is 'to break down discriminatory attitudes and cultural jealousies'. This goal seeks to enhance mutual acceptance among all cultural groups, and is to be approached through two main programme components. One is the *cultural* component, which is to be achieved by providing support and encouragement for cultural maintenance and development among all cultural groups in the plural society. The other is the *social* or *intercultural* component, which promotes the sharing of cultural expressions by providing opportunities for intergroup contact, and the removal of barriers to full and equitable participation in the daily life of the larger society. (A third component acknowledges the importance of learning a common language(s) in order to permit intercultural participation among all groups.) In short, the 1971 Canadian policy proposed that both diversity and equitable participation are at the core of the meaning of multiculturalism. It is perhaps no coincidence that these two principles are the same as the two dimensions in the acculturation strategies framework!

Following up on ideas in this policy statement, we (Berry et al., 1977) carried out a national survey to empirically examine these core elements of multiculturalism, including knowledge and conceptions of multiculturalism, attitudes towards the policy and multicultural ideology. This last concept was defined as the acceptance and importance of maintaining cultural diversity and of equitable participation by all groups and individuals in Canadian society. These two components are, of course, the two issues addressed in the acculturation strategies framework. We found a generally high level of support for multiculturalism (Berry & Kalin, 1995). Since then, we (Berry, 2013a, 2016) have continued to monitor the acceptance of multiculturalism using the Multiculturalism Ideology scale and other instruments (using some items from the original scale). In general, support remains high, and along with immigration, multiculturalism continues to be accepted as one of the defining characteristics of Canadian society. As revealed in a recent survey: 'The latest Focus Canada survey – updating trends dating back to the 1980s – shows that Canadian attitudes about these issues has held steady or grown more positive over the past three to five years. The public continues to believe that immigration is good for the economy, and are more confident than before about the country's ability to manage refugees . . . . . . Multiculturalism continues to be seen as one of the country's most important symbols, and this view has strengthened since 2010' (Environics Institute, 2015/2018).

Numerous studies (in collaboration with students) have continued this research on acculturation in Canada. These include studies of: immigrants from Korea (Kim & Berry, 1985; Kwak & Berry, 2001), Greece (Georgas, Berry & Shaw, 1996; Sands & Berry, 1993), Turkey (Ataca & Berry, 2002; Aycan & Berry, 1996) and North Africa and Haiti (Berry & Sabatier, 2010); refugees from Central America (Dona & Berry, 1994) and Vietnam (Berry & Blondel, 1982) and sojourners from China (Chataway & Berry, 1989; Gui, Safdar & Berry, 2016; Zheng & Berry, 1991). Other student thesis projects (not published) have been with immigrant communities, such as Portuguese, Indians, Chinese and Jamaicans in Canada. Most recently, we (Berry & Hou, 2016, 2017, 2019) have used the large database from the Social Survey by Statistics Canada to examine the acculturation of first- and second-generation immigrants to Canada from a variety of countries around the world. In all these studies, we have examined the impact of acculturation on the lives of peoples following their migration to Canada, using the concepts and measures (strategies and adaptation) outlined earlier. As with other studies, those using the integration strategy reported the highest levels of wellbeing, and those with a marginalization strategy had the lowest levels.

The cross-cultural perspective warns us that the research findings in Canada (or any other single country) cannot serve as a basis for any general claims for the outcomes of intercultural contact. As noted earlier, the Canadian political, historical and policy context is unique (Adams, 2007). This is an approach that is avowedly pluralist, even to the extent that the prime minister (Foran, 2017) has asserted that there is no 'mainstream' in Canada. As noted earlier, in keeping with this perspective, my own research has avoided the use of this term, preferring the notion of 'larger society'. Similarly, many researchers in Canada avoid the use of the term 'minority', preferring instead to use the concepts of 'cultural community' and 'ethnocultural group' in recognition of the groups' cultures. However, in an example of scientific acculturation, these terms are sometimes used as a result of the dominant position of US social and behavioural science.

In order to examine these phenomena beyond Canada, and to search for some possible universals of acculturation, we have examined acculturation in China, with migrant workers moving from rural farming to urban industrial communities (Gui et al., 2012) and refugees from the 2008 earthquake in Sechuan to safe cities (Han, Zheng & Berry, 2016). From my position at the National Research University, Centre for Sociocultural Research in Moscow, in close collaboration with colleagues there, I have been examining the acculturation and adaptation of various groups of immigrants and ethnocultural groups in Russia (Berry, 2017; Lebedeva, Tatarko & Berry, 2016) and some groups of Russians in other countries, such as in Estonia (Kruusvall et al., 2009), Germany (Schmitz & Berry, 2009) and Belgium (Grigoryev & Berry, 2017).

6.3 International Projects: The ICSEY and MIRIPS Projects

Two international projects have examined a variety of acculturating groups within a shared research framework that focuses on acculturation and intercultural relations. These are the International Comparative Study of Ethnocultural Youth (ICSEY; Berry et al., 2006a, 2006b) and the Mutual Intercultural Relations in Plural Societies (MIRIPS; Berry, 2017) projects. These studies were carried out in collaboration with numerous colleagues in these societies of settlement.

The first project sampled more than 5,000 immigrant and ethnocultural youth from 32 societies who had settled in 13 countries. This project examined youths' experience of acculturation, particularly their strategies and adaptations, and the relationships between these two features of psychological acculturation. We found that there were four acculturation profiles that closely matched the four acculturation strategies; those in the integration profile had the best psychological and sociocultural adaptation, and those in the marginalization profile (called 'diffuse' in that study) had the worst adaptation outcomes. This conclusion was confirmed in a re-analysis of the ICSEY data by Abu-Rayya and Sam (2017). We conclude that the generalization made by Berry (1997b) and confirmed in the meta-analysis by Nguyen and Benet-Martínez (2013) is valid: the integration strategy generally provides the best route to a successful life in a new society.

The second project (MIRIPS; Berry, 2017) included samples of both dominant and non-dominant groups in 17 societies; some were immigrants, some were sojourners and some were members of ethnocultural groups. This sampling strategy was designed to examine their *mutual* acculturation and intercultural relations in order to discover if these groups share any general principles. We sought to evaluate the three hypotheses (multiculturalism, integration and contact) outlined earlier. We found substantial support for these three hypotheses (between 85 per cent and 92 per cent of evaluations), and concluded that there are indeed some general principles of acculturation and intercultural relations. In no case did a lack of security (and the presence of discrimination) lead to mutual positive attitudes. In no case did marginalization lead to better psychological and sociocultural adaptation. And in no case did barriers to intercultural contact lead to more positive mutual regard.

Note that the data from these two international projects have been analysed in different ways. The ICSEY data were collected with a standard research instrument, with similar samples (immigrant youth and their parents). This permitted the data to be brought together into a single database, on which equivalence could be assessed and comparisons made across groups and societies. In the MIRIPS project, however, although there was a common research instrument with a standard set of variables, the unique intercultural situation in each society, and different kinds of samples, meant that the variables were operationalized somewhat differently across countries. In this case, there was no attempt to create a single data base and hence no equivalence or direct comparisons could be carried out.

Despite these differences in analytic strategy, in both these international projects, we sought to discover if there are any general principles of acculturation and intercultural relations that may be *universal*. By universal, I mean the existence of basic processes or capacities that are shared by all individuals and that become shaped by cultural and intercultural experiences during development into differential expressions. These underlying similarities serve as the necessary basis for intercultural interactions; without them there would be no possibility that individuals or groups could have meaningful relationships across cultures. And without them there could be no comparisons of cultures and individuals; this is because some communalities are required in order to make valid comparisons.

7 Conclusion

In this Element, I have attempted to portray some of the issues, concepts and empirical findings in the field of acculturation, mainly using my own involvement and experience. No attempt has been made to portray the whole field; this would be impossible in a short document such as this, and may indeed be impossible at present, even in a full-length book. The increase in conceptual and empirical materials in the past 50 years puts such a comprehensive goal beyond reach of any one author or publication.

Nevertheless, I believe that the materials presented and reviewed in this Element are of some value to students and researchers in acculturation. Since all scholarship is personal and political, I have added my own voice and perspectives to this domain, and invite others to do the same.

The future of the field is now in the hands, increasingly, of scholars from all over the world. From a beginning in anthropology concerned with managing colonization by the West, and in sociology concerned with problems of migration to the West, many scholars from many disciplines from other societies are taking charge of the field. They are making acculturation research more culturally sensitive and socially relevant to contemporary issues, particularly to the plight of refugees, to reconciliation with Indigenous Peoples and to reducing the marginalization and exclusion of those without power and resources in our increasingly economically and politically divisive societies.

I look forward to advances in the field that will take us all beyond the current limited state of knowledge and action.

References

Abu-Rayya, H. & Sam, D. L. (2017). Is integration the best way to acculturate? A re-examination of the bicultural–adaptation relationship in the 'ICSEY dataset' using the bilineal method. *Journal of Cross-Cultural Psychology, 48*, 287–93.

Adams, M. (2007). *Unlikely utopia: The surprising triumph of Canadian pluralism*. Toronto: Viking.

Allport, G. W. (1954). *The nature of prejudice*. Reading, MA: Addison-Wesley.

Ataca, B. (1998). Psychological, sociocultural and marital adaptation of Turkish immigrants in Canada. PhD thesis, Queen's University.

Ataca, B. & Berry, J. W. (2002). Psychological, sociocultural and marital adaptation of Turkish immigrant couples in Canada. *International Journal of Psychology, 37*, 13–26.

Aycan, Z. & Berry, J. W. (1996). Impact of employment-related experiences on immigrants' psychological well-being and adaptation to Canada. *Canadian Journal of Behavioural Science, 28*, 240–51.

Benet-Martínez, V. & Haritatos, J. (2005). Factor structure and factorial invariance of the Multidimensional Acculturative Stress Inventory. *Journal of Personality, 73*, 1015–50.

Berry, J. W. (1966a). Cultural determinants of perception. PhD thesis, University of Edinburgh, Scotland.

Berry, J. W. (1966b). Temne and Eskimo perceptual skills. *International Journal of Psychology, 1*, 207–29.

Berry, J. W. (1967). Independence and conformity in subsistence-level societies. *Journal of Personality and Social Psychology, 7*, 415–18.

Berry, J. W. (1969). On cross-cultural comparability. *International Journal of Psychology, 4* 119–28.

Berry, J. W. (1970). Marginality, stress and ethnic identification in an acculturated Aboriginal community. *Journal of Cross-Cultural Psychology, 1*, 239–52.

Berry, J. W. (1971). Ecological and cultural factors in spatial perceptual development. *Canadian Journal of Behavioural Science, 3*, 324-36.

Berry, J. W. (1972). Radical cultural relativism and the concept of intelligence. In. L. J. Cronbach and P. Drenth (eds.) *Mental tests and cultural adaptation*, (pp. 77-88). Den Haag: Mouton.

Berry, J. W. (1974a). Psychological aspects of cultural pluralism: Unity and identity reconsidered. *Topics in Culture Learning, 2*, 17–22.

Berry, J. W. (1974b. Differentiation across cultures: Cognitive style and affective style. In J. L. M. Dawson & W. J. Lonner (eds.), *Cross-cultural psychology* (pp. 167–75). Hong Kong: University of Hong Kong Press.

Berry, J. W. (1976). *Human ecology and cognitive style: Comparative studies in cultural and psychological adaptation*. New York: Sage/Halsted.

Berry, J. W. (1977). Acculturative stress among the James Bay Cree: Prelude to a hydroelectric project. In L. Muller-Wille, P. Pelto, Li. Muller-Wille & R. Darnell (eds.), *Consequences of economic change in circumpolar regions* (pp. 105–19). Edmonton: Boreal Institute.

Berry, J. W. (1979). A cultural ecology of social behaviour. In L. Berkowitz (ed.), *Advances in experimental social psychology*, Vol. 12 (pp. 177-206). New York: Academic Press.

Berry, J. W. (1980b). Social and cultural change. In H. C. Triandis & R. Brislin (eds.), *Handbook of cross-cultural psychology, Vol. 5, Social psychology* (pp. 211–79). Boston, MA: Allyn and Bacon.

Berry, J. W. (1980a). Acculturation as varieties of adaptation. In A. Padilla (ed.), *Acculturation: Theory, models and some new findings* (pp. 9–25). Boulder, CO: Westview.

Berry, J. W. (1989). Imposed etics, emics, derived etics: The operationalization of a compelling idea. *International Journal of Psychology*, *24*, 721–35.

Berry, J. W. (1992). Acculturation and adaptation in a new society. *International Migration*, *30*, 69–85.

Berry, J. W. (1995). The descendants of a model. *Culture and Psychology*, *1*, 373–80.

Berry, J. W. (1997a). Cruising the world: A nomad in academe. In M. H. Bond (ed.), *Working at the interface of cultures* (pp. 138–53). London: Routledge.

Berry, J. W. (1997b). Immigration, acculturation and adaptation. (Lead article with commentary). *Applied Psychology: An International Review*, *46*, 5–68.

Berry, J. W. (1999). Aboriginal cultural identity. *Canadian Journal of Native Studies*, *19*, 1–36.

Berry, J. W. (2001). A psychology of immigration. *Journal of Social Issues*, *57*, 615–31.

Berry, J. W. (2003). Conceptual approaches to acculturation. In K. Chun, P. Balls-Organista & G. Marin (eds.), *Acculturation: Theory, method and applications* (pp. 17–37). Washington, DC: American Psychological Association.

Berry, J. W. (2006a). Stress perspectives on acculturation In D. Sam & J. W. Berry (eds.), *Cambridge handbook of acculturation psychology* (pp. 43–57). Cambridge: Cambridge University Press.

Berry, J. W. (2006b). Design of acculturation studies. In D. Sam & J. W. Berry (eds.), *Cambridge handbook of acculturation psychology* (pp. 129–41). Cambridge: Cambridge University Press.

Berry, J. W. (2008). Globalisation and acculturation. *International Journal of Intercultural Relations*, *32*, 328–36.

Berry, J. W. (2009). A critique of critical acculturation. *International Journal of Intercultural Relations*, *33*, 361–71.

Berry, J. W. (2013b). Achieving a global psychology. *Canadian Psychology*, *54*, 55–61.

Berry, J. W. (2013a). Research on multiculturalism in Canada. *International Journal of Intercultural Relations*, *37*, 663–75.

Berry, J. W. (2015). Intercultural adaptation. Paper presented to Canadian Psychological Association Conference. Toronto, Canada.

Berry, J. W. (2016). Comparative analysis of Canadian multiculturalism policy and the multiculturalism policies of other countries. *Psychology in Russia State of the Art*, *9*, 4–23.

Berry, J. W. (2017). Theories and models of acculturation. In S. J. Schwartz & J. Ungar (eds.). *Oxford handbook of acculturation and health* (pp. 15–28). Oxford: Oxford University Press.

Berry, J. W. (2018). Ecological perspective on human behaviour. In A. Uskul & S. Oishi (eds.). *Socio-economic environment and human psychology* (pp. 3–32). Oxford: Oxford University Press.

Berry, J. W. (2019). Diversity and equity in plural societies. In J. Pandey, R. Kumar & K. Thapa (eds.).*Psychological perspectives on diversity and social development* (pp. 23–36). Singapore: Springer Nature.

Berry, J. W. & Bennett, J. (1989). Syllabic literacy and cognitive performance among the Cree. *International Journal of Psychology*, *24*, 429–50.

Berry, J. W. & Bennett, J. A. (1992). Cree conceptions of cognitive competence. *International Journal of Psychology*, *27*, 73–88.

Berry, J. W. & Blondel, T. (1982). Psychological adaptation of Vietnamese refugees in Canada. *Canadian Journal of Community Mental Health*, *1*, 81–8.

Berry, J. W. & Hou, F. (2016). Immigrant acculturation and wellbeing in Canada. *Canadian Psychology*, *57*, 254–64.

Berry, J. W. & Hou, F. (2017) Acculturation, discrimination and wellbeing among second generation of immigrants in Canada. *International Journal of Intercultural Relations*, *61*, 29–39.

Berry, J. W. & Hou, F. (2019). Multiple belongings and psychological wellbeing among immigrants and the second generation in Canada *Canadian Journal of Behavioural Science*, *51*, 159–70.

Berry, J. W. & Kalin, R. (1995). Multicultural and ethnic attitudes in Canada: Overview of the 1991 survey. *Canadian Journal of Behavioural Science*, *27*, 301–20.

Berry, J. W. & Kalin, R. (2000). Multicultural policy and social psychology: The Canadian experience. In S. Renshon & J. Duckitt (eds.), *Political psychology in cross-cultural perspective* (pp. 263–84). New York: MacMillan.

Berry, J. W., Kalin, R. & Taylor, D. M. (1977). *Multiculturalism and ethnic attitudes in Canada*. Ottawa: Government of Canada.

Berry, J. W., Kim, U., Minde, T. & Mok, D. (1987). Comparative studies of acculturative stress. *International Migration Review*, *21*, 491–511.

Berry, J. W., Kim, U., Power, S., Young, M. & Bujaki, M. (1989). Acculturation attitudes in plural societies. *Applied Psychology: An International Review*, *38*, 185–296.

Berry, J. W., Phinney, J., Sam, D. & Vedder, P. (eds.). (2006a). *Immigrant youth in cultural transition: Acculturation, identity and adaptation across national contexts*. Mahwah, NJ: Lawrence Erlbaum Associates.

Berry, J. W., Phinney, J. S., Sam, D. L. & Vedder, P. (2006b). Immigrant youth: Acculturation, identity and adaptation. *Applied Psychology: An International Review*, *55*, 303–32.

Berry, J. W., Poortinga, Y. H., Breugelmans, S., Chasiotis, A. & Sam, D. L. (2011). *Cross-cultural psychology: Research and applications* (3rd ed.). Cambridge: Cambridge University Press.

Berry, J. W., Poortinga, Y. H., Segall, M. H. & Dasen, P. R. (1992). *Cross-cultural psychology: Research and applications*. New York: Cambridge University Press.

Berry, J. W., Poortinga, Y. H., Segall, M. H. & Dasen, P. R. (2002). *Cross-cultural psychology: Research and applications* (2nd ed.). New York: Cambridge University Press.

Berry, J. W. & Sabatier, C. (2010). Acculturation, discrimination, and adaptation among second generation immigrant youth in Montreal and Paris. *International Journal of Intercultural Relations*, *34*, 191–207.

Berry, J. W. & Sabatier, C. (2011). Variations in the assessment of acculturation attitudes: Their relationships with psychological wellbeing. *International Journal of Intercultural Relations*, *35*, 658–69.

Berry, J. W. & Sam, D. L. (2016). Theoretical perspectives. In D. L. Sam & J. W. Berry (eds.), *Cambridge handbook of acculturation psychology* (2nd ed.) (pp. 11–29). Cambridge: Cambridge University Press.

Berry, J. W., Trimble, J. & Olmeda, E. (1986). The assessment of acculturation. In W. J. Lonner & J. W. Berry (eds.), *Field methods in cross-cultural research* (pp. 291–324). London: Sage Publications.

Berry, J. W., van de Koppel, J. M. H., Sénéchal, C., Annis, R. C., Bahuchet, S., Cavalli-Sforza, L. L. & Witkin, H. A. (1986). *On the edge of the forest: Cultural adaptation and cognitive development in Central Africa*. Lisse: Swets and Zeitlinger.

Berry, J. W., Wintrob, R. M., Sindell, P. S. & Mawhinney, T. A. (1982). Psychological adaptation to culture change among the James Bay Cree. *Naturaliste Canadien*, *109*, 965–75.

Bourhis, R., Moïse, C., Perrault, S. & Sénécal, S. (1997). Towards an interactive acculturation model: A social psychological approach. *International Journal of Psychology*, *32*, 369–86.

Boyd, R. & Richerson, P. J. (1983). Why is culture adaptive? *Quarterly Review of Biology*, *58*, 209–14.

Boyd, R. & Richerson, P. J. (2005). *The origin and evolution of cultures*. New York: Oxford University Press.

Boyd, R., Richerson, P. J., & Henrich, J. (2011). The cultural niche: Why social learning is essential for human adaptation. *Proceedings of the National Academy of Sciences* (USA), *108*(2), 10918–25.

Breton, C. (2019). Do incorporation policies matter? Immigrants' identity and relationships with the receiving society. *Comparative Political Studies*, 1–32. doi:10.1177/0010414019830708

Bronfenbrenner, U. (1979). *The ecology of human development*. Cambridge, MA: Harvard University Press.

Cawte, J. (1972). *Cruel, poor and brutal nations*. Honolulu: Hawaii University Press.

Chataway, C. & Berry, J. W. (1989). Acculturation experiences, appraisal, coping and adaptation: A comparison of Hong Kong Chinese, French and English students in Canada. *Canadian Journal of Behavioural Science*, *21*, 295–309.

Chirkov, V. I. (2009). Critical psychology of acculturation: What do we study and how do we study it, when we investigate acculturation. *International Journal of Intercultural Relations*, *33*, 94–105.

Chun, K., Balls-Organista, P. & Marin, G. (eds.) (2003). *Acculturation: Theory, method and applications*. Washington, DC: American Psychological Association.

Darwin, C. (1859). *On the origin of species*. New York: Random House.

Dona, G. (1990). Acculturation and mental health of Central American refugees in Canada. MA thesis, Queen's University.

Dona, G. & Berry, J. W. (1994). Acculturation attitudes and acculturative stress of Central American refugees in Canada. *International Journal of Psychology*, *29*, 57–70.

Environics Institute (2015/2018). *Focus Canada: 2015 survey on immigration and multiculturalism*. Toronto: Environics Institute.

Fagan, B. & Durani, N. (2016). *People of the earth: An introduction to world prehistory* (14th ed.). London: Routledge.

Feldman, D. A. (1975). The history of the relationship between environment and culture in ethnological thought. *Journal of the History of the Behavioural Sciences*, *110*, 67–81.

Ferguson, G. M. & Bornstein, M. H. (2012). Remote acculturation: The 'Americanization' of Jamaican Islanders. *International Journal of Behavioral Development*, 36(3), 167–77.

Foran, C. (2017). The Canada experiment: Is this the world's first 'postnational' country? *The Guardian*. www.theguardian.com/world/2017/jan/04/the-canada-experiment-is-this-the-worlds-first-postnational-country

Forde, D. (1934). *Habitat, economy and society*. New York: Dutton.

Geertz, C. (1973). *The interpretation of cultures*. New York: Basic Books.

Georgas, J., Berry, J. W. & Shaw, A. (1996). Acculturation of Greek family values. *Journal of Cross-Cultural Psychology*, *27*, 329–38.

Georgas, J., Berry, J. W., van de Vijver, F., Kagitcibasi, C. & Poortinga, Y. H. (eds.) (2006). *Family structure and function: A 30 nation psychological study*. Cambridge: Cambridge University Press.

Gezentsvey-Lamy, M., Ward, C. & and Liu, J. (2013). Motivation for ethno-cultural continuity. *Journal of Cross-Cultural Psychology*, *44*, 147–66.

Government of Canada (1971). *Statement on multiculturalism*. Ottawa: Hansard.

Graves, T. D. (1967). Psychological acculturation in a tri-ethnic community. *Southwestern Journal of Anthropology*, *23*, 337–50.

Grigoryev, D. & Berry, J. W. (2017). Acculturation preferences, ethnic and religious identification and the socio-economic adaptation of Russian-speaking immigrants in Belgium. *Journal of Intercultural Communication Research*, *46*, 537–57.

Gui, Y., Safdar, S. & Berry, J. W. (2016). Mutual intercultural relations among university students in Canada. *Frontiers: The Interdisciplinary Journal of Study Abroad*, *27*, 17–32.

Gui, Y., Zheng, Y. & Berry, J. W. (2012). Migrant worker acculturation in China. *International Journal of Intercultural Relations*, *36*, 598–610.

Han, L., Zheng, Y. & Berry, J. W. (2016). Differences in resilience by acculturation strategies: A study with Qiang nationality following the 2008 Chinese earthquake. *International Journal of Emergency Mental Health*, *17*, 573–80.

Harris, M. (1968). *The rise of anthropological theory: A history of theories of culture*. New York: Thomas Y. Cromwell Company.

Haugen, I. & Kunst, J. R. (2017) A two-way process? A qualitative and quantitative investigation of majority members' acculturation. *International Journal of Intercultural Relations*, *60*, 67–82.

Huntington, E. (1945). *Mainsprings of civilization*. New York: John Wiley.

Igarashi, A. (2019). Till multiculturalism do us part: Multicultural policies and the national identification of immigrants in European countries. *Social Science Research*, *77*, 88–100.

Inkeles, A. & Smith, D. (1974). *Becoming modern*. Cambridge, MA: Harvard University Press.

Jahoda, G. (1995). The ancestry of a model. *Culture and Psychology*, *1*, 11–24.

Kalin, R. & Berry, J. W. (1982). Social ecology of ethnic attitudes in Canada. *Canadian Journal of Behavioural Science*, *14*, 97-109.

Kalin, R. & Berry, J. W. (1995). Ethnic and civic self-identity in Canada: Analyses of 1974 and 1991 national surveys. *Canadian Ethnic Studies*, *27*, 1–15.

Kardiner, A. & Linton, R. (1939). *The individual and his society.* New York: Colombia University Press.

Keller, H. (2002). Development as the interface between biology and culture. A conceptualization of early ontogenetic experiences. In H. Keller, Y. Poortinga & A. Schoelmerich (eds.), *Between culture and biology* (pp. 215–40). Cambridge: Cambridge University Press.

Keller, H. (2011). Biology, culture and development. In F. van de Vijver, A. Chastiotis & S. Breugelmans (eds.), *Fundamental questions in cross-cultural psychology* (pp. 312–40). Cambridge: Cambridge University Press.

Kim, U. and Berry, J. W. (1985). Acculturation attitudes of Korean immigrant in Canada. In I. Reyes-Lagunes & Y. Poortinga (eds.), *From a Different Perspective* (pp. 93–105). Lisse: Swets and Zeitlinger.

Kruusvall, J., Vetik, R. & Berry, J. W. (2009). The strategies of inter-ethnic adaptation of Estonian Russians. *Studies of Transition States and Societies*, *1*, 3–24.

Kwak, K. & Berry, J. W. (2001). Generational differences in acculturation among Asian families in Canada. *International Journal of Psychology*, *36*, 152–62.

Lalonde, R. & Cameron, J. (1993). An intergroup perspective on immigrant acculturation with a focus on collective strategies. *International Journal of Psychology*, *28*, 57–74.

Lazarus, R. (1997). Acculturation isn't everything. *Applied Psychology: An International Review*, *46*, 39–43.

Lazarus, R. & Folkman, S. (1984). *Stress, appraisal and coping*. New York: Springer.

Lebedeva, N. & Tatarko, A. (2013). Multiculturalism and immigration in post-Soviet Russia. *European Psychologist*, *18*, 169–78.

Lebedeva, N., Tatarko, A. & Berry, J. (2016). Intercultural relations in Russia and Latvia: The relationship between contact and cultural security. *Psychology in Russia: State of the Art*, *9*(1), pp. 39–54. doi:10.11621/pir.2016.0103

Liebkind, K. (2001). Acculturation. In R. Brown & S. Gaertner (eds.), *Blackwell handbook of social psychology: Intergroup processes* (pp. 386–406). Oxford: Blackwell.

Masgoret, A.-M., & Ward, C. (2006). The cultural learning approach to acculturation. In D. L. Sam & J. W. Berry (eds.), *Cambridge handbook of acculturation psychology* (pp. 58–77). Cambridge: Cambridge University Press.

Mena, J., Padilla, A. & Maldonado, M. (1987). Acculturative stress and specific coping strategies among immigrant and later generation college students. *Hispanic Journal of Behavioural Sciences*. https://doi.org/10.1177/07399863870092006

Mishra, R. C. & Berry, J. W. (2017). *Ecology, culture and human development: Lessons for Adivasi education*. New Delhi: Sage Publications.

Mishra, R. C., Sinha, D. & Berry, J. W. (1996). *Ecology, acculturation and psychological adaptation among Adivasi in India*. Delhi: Sage Publications.

Moghaddam, F. M. (1988). Individualistic and collective integration strategies among immigrants. In J. W. Berry & R. C. Annis (eds.), *Ethnic psychology* (pp. 69–79). Amsterdam: Swets & Zeitlinger.

Moran, E. (2006). *People and nature: An introduction to human ecological relations* (3rd ed.). Malden, MA: Blackwell Publishing.

Navas, M., García, M. C., Sánchez, J., Rojas, A. J., Pumares, P. & Fernández, J. S. (2005). Relative acculturation extended model (RAEM). *International Journal of Intercultural Relations*, *29*, 21–37.

Nguyen, A.-M. & Benet-Martínez, V. (2013). Biculturalism and adjustment: A meta-analysis. *Journal of Cross-Cultural Psychology* *44*(1), 122–59.

Oberg, K. (1960). Cultural shock: Adjustment to new cultural environments. *Practical Anthropology*, *7*, 177-82.

Padilla, A. (1980) (ed.), *Acculturation: Theory, models and some new findings*. Boulder, CO: Westview.

Pettigrew, T. & Tropp, L. (2011). *When groups meet*. London: Psychology Press.

Pruegger, V. (1993). Aboriginal and non-Aboriginal work values. PhD thesis, Queen's University.

Redfield, R., Linton, R. & Herskovits, M. J. (1936). Memorandum on the study of acculturation. *American Anthropologist*, *38*, 149–52.

Richardson, B. (1974). *Strangers devour the land.* Toronto: Douglas & McIntyre.

Rodriguez, N., Myers, H. F., Mira, C. B., Flores, T., & Garcia-Hernandez, L. (2002). Development of the Multidimensional Acculturative Stress Inventory for adults of Mexican origin. *Psychological Assessment, 14*, 451–61.

Rudmin, F. W. (2009). Catalogue of acculturation constructs: Descriptions of 126 taxonomies, 1918–2003. *Online Readings in Psychology and Culture, 8*(1). https://doi.org/10.9707/2307–0919.1074

Safdar, S., Choung, K., & Lewis, J. R. (2013).A review of the MIDA model and other contemporary acculturation models. In E. Tartakovsky (ed.), *Immigration: Policies, challenges and impact* (pp. 213–30). Hauppauge, NY: Nova Science Publishers.

Sam, D. L. & Berry, J. W. (2013). Acculturation: When individuals and groups of different cultural backgrounds meet. *Perspectives on Psychological Science, 5*(4), 472–81.

Sam, D. L. & Berry, J. W. (eds.) (2006/2016). *The Cambridge handbook of acculturation psychology.* New York: Cambridge University Press.

Sands, E. & Berry, J. W. (1993). Acculturation and mental health among Greek-Canadians in Toronto. *Canadian Journal of Community Mental Health, 12*, 117–24.

Schmitz, P. & Berry, J. W. (2009). Structure of acculturation attitudes and their relationships with personality and psychological adaptation: A study with immigrant and national samples in Germany. In K. Boehnke (ed.), *Proceedings of IACCP Congress*. www.iaccp.org/Bremen

Schönpflug, U. (ed.) (2009). *Cultural transmission: Developmental, psychological, social and methodological perspectives*. Cambridge: Cambridge University Press.

Schwartz, S. & Unger, J. (2017). *Oxford handbook of acculturation and health.* New York: Oxford University Press.

Searle, W. & Ward, C. (1990). The prediction of psychological and socio-cultural adjustment during cross-cultural transitions. *International Journal of Inter-cultural Relations, 14*, 449–64.

Segall, M. H., Dasen, P. R., Berry, J. W. & Poortinga, Y. H. (1990). *Human behavior in global perspective: An introduction to cross-cultural psychology.* New York: Pergamon.

Segall, M. H., Dasen, P. R., Berry, J. W. & Poortinga, Y. H. (1999). *Human behavior in global perspective* (2nd ed.) Boston: Allyn & Bacon.

Sinha, D. (1978). Story-pictorial E.F.T.: A culturally appropriate test of perceptual disembedding. *Indian Journal of Psychology, 53*(2), 160–71.

Snauwaert, B., Soenens, B., Vanbeselaere, N. & Boen, F. (2003). When integration does not necessarily imply integration. Different conceptualizations of acculturation orientations lead to different classifications. *Journal of Cross-Cultural Psychology*, *3*, 231–9.

Social Science Research Council (USA) (1954). Acculturation: An exploratory formulation. *American Anthropologist*, *56*, 973–1002.

Sommerlad, E. & Berry, J. W. (1970). The role of ethnic identification in distinguishing between attitudes towards assimilation and integration of a minority racial group. *Human Relations*, *23*, 23–9.

Stephan, W., Renfro, C. L., Esses, V., Stephan, C. & Martin, T. (2005). The effects of feeling threatened on attitudes toward immigrants. *International Journal of Intercultural Relations*, *29*, 1–19.

Super, C. & Harkness, S. (1986). The developmental niche: A conceptualisation at the interface of childhood and culture. *International Journal of Behavioural Development*, *9*, 545–69.

Super, C. & Harkness, S. (1997). The cultural structuring of child development. J. W. Berry, P. R. Dasen & T. S. Saraswathi (eds.), *Handbook of cross-cultural psychology, Vol. 2. Basic processes and human development* (pp. 1–39). Boston: Allyn & Bacon.

Thurnwald, R. (1932). The psychology of acculturation. *American Anthropologist*, *34*, 557–69.

Townsend, P. (2009). People and nature: An introduction to human ecological relations. *Australian Journal of Anthropology*, *20*, 392–3.

Van de Vijver, F., Celenk, O. & Berry, J. W. (2016). Research design and assessment of acculturation. In D. L. Sam & J. W. Berry (eds.). *Cambridge handbook of acculturation psychology* (2nd ed.) (pp. 71–92). Cambridge: Cambridge University Press.

Van de Vijver, F. J. R. & Leung, K. (1997). *Methods and data analysis for cross-cultural research*. Newbury Park, CA: Sage Publications.

Van Oudenhoven, J. P. & Ward, C. (2013). Fading majority cultures: The implications of transnationalism and demographic changes for immigrant acculturation. *Journal of Community and Applied Social Psychology*, 23(2), 81–97.

Vayda, A. & Rappaport, R. (1968). Ecology: Cultural and non-cultural. In J. Clifton (ed.), *Introduction to cultural anthropology*. (pp. 477–97). Boston: Houghton Mifflin.

Ward, C. (2001). The ABCs of acculturation. In D. Matsumoto (ed.), *The handbook of culture and psychology* (pp. 411–45). Oxford: Oxford University Press.

Ward, C. (2008). Thinking outside the Berry boxes. *International Journal of Intercultural Relations*, *32*, 114–23.

Ward, C., Bochner, S. & Furnham, A. (2001). *The psychology of culture shock*. Hove: Routledge.

Ward, C. & Masgoret, A.-M. (2008). Attitudes toward immigrants, immigration, and multiculturalism in New Zealand: A social psychological analysis. *International Migration Review*, 42, 227–48.

Weisner, T. (1984). A cross-cultural perspective: Ecocultural niches in middle childhood. In A. Collins (ed.), *The elementary school years* (pp. 335–69). Washington, DC: Academic Press.

Whiting, B. B. & Whiting, J. W. (1975). *Children of six cultures: A psychocultural analysis*. Cambridge, MA: Harvard University Press.

Wilson, J., Ward, C., Velichko, H. & Bethel, R. (2017). Measuring cultural competencies: The development and validation of a revised measure of sociocultural adaptation. *Journal of Cross-Cultural Psychology*, 48, 1475–1506.

Yerkes, R., Bridges, J. W. & Hardwick, R. (1917). A point scale for measuring mental ability. *Journal of Philosophy, Psychology and Scientific Methods*, *14*, 330–3.

Zheng, X. & Berry, J. W. (1991). Psychological adaptation of Chinese sojourners in Canada. *International Journal of Psychology*, *26*, 451–70.

Acknowledgements

This Element is dedicated to Joan, my wife, who has tolerated my wanderings around the globe in my search of knowledge and pleasure.

I thank Walt Lonner and David Sam for their helpful comments on a draft of this Element.

This Element was prepared within the framework of the HSE University Basic Research Program and funded by the Russian Academic Excellence Project '5-100'.

Cambridge Elements

Psychology and Culture

Kenneth D. Keith
University of San Diego
Kenneth D. Keith is author or editor of more than 160 publications on cross-cultural psychology, quality of life, intellectual disability, and the teaching of psychology. He was the 2017 president of the Society for the Teaching of Psychology.

About the Series

Elements in Psychology and Culture features authoritative surveys and updates on key topics in cultural, cross-cultural, and indigenous psychology. Authors are internationally recognized scholars whose work is at the forefront of their subdisciplines within the realm of psychology and culture.

Cambridge Elements

Psychology and Culture

Elements in the Series

The Continuing Growth of Cross-Cultural Psychology: A First-Person Annotated Chronology
Walter J. Lonner

Measuring and Interpreting Subjective Wellbeing in Different Cultural Contexts: A Review and Way Forward
Robert A. Cummins

The Nature and Challenges of Indigenous Psychologies
Carl Martin Allwood

Global Changes in Children's Lives
Uwe P. Gielen and Sunghun Kim

Gene–Culture Interactions: Toward an Explanatory Framework
Joni Y. Sasaki and Heewon Kwon

Culture-inclusive Theories: An Epistemological Strategy
Kwang-Kuo Hwang

Acculturation: A Personal Journey across Cultures
John W. Berry

A full series listing is available at: www.cambridge.org/EPAC

Printed in the United States
By Bookmasters